MAXIMUM TIER ONE:

Improving

Full-Class Instruction

- Pat Quinn -

The RTI Guy

Maximum Tier One:

Improving Full-Class Instruction

Pat Quinn

Copyright© 2012 Pat Quinn

ISBN 9780-9838516-2-2

JULIANJOHN

JulianJohn Publishing

Cover Design by Sean O'Connor
OhSeeDesign.com

Printed in the United States of America

TABLE OF CONTENTS

INTRODUCTION

Greetings from "The RTI Guy"!

For the past five years, I have helped teachers around the country implement Response to Intervention in their schools and districts. My seminars, books, and newsletter have reached hundreds of thousands of teachers and have had an impact on the education that millions of students receive each day.

During this process, one fact became very clear:

> **The first step to successfully implementing Response to Intervention is to provide Outstanding Full Class Instruction to every student.**

This full class instruction is usually referred to as "Tier One" in an RTI system. My RTI newsletter has over 20,000 subscribers, and by far the most common question I receive from readers is: "How do we improve full class instruction?"

This book is one step of that process. It will provide you with tools, strategies, techniques, and instructional models to increase learning and success in your classroom. It will not solve every problem or eliminate the need for Tier Two or Tier Three in your RTI system, but it will help you maximize the instruction in class every day.

What you will find in this book:

Chapter 1: Four Directions

Before instruction can be effective, students need to be moving in the right direction. Actually, they need to be moving in the right "Four Directions." This chapter will explain the four directions you need to move your students toward in order to maximize full-class instruction.

Chapter 2: Teaching Individual Differences

Outstanding instruction requires that different students in your class do different activities at the same time. This is often referred to as "differentiated instruction." This is not possible until your students have a firm understanding of individual student differences.

Chapter 3: Essential Lesson Components

Every lesson has certain components that must be present to maximize instruction. This chapter will go over each of these components with an emphasis on getting the most out of every minute of full classroom instruction.

Chapter 4: Five Opportunities

Every lesson has five opportunities to maximize instruction built right into it. This chapter will show you those five opportunities and how you can use them to increase student learning each day.

Chapter 6: Five Models of Instruction

How you design your lessons can make the difference! This chapter will show you five different models you can use to meet the individual learning needs of the students in your class each day.

Chapter 7: Putting It All Together

Continual improvement is the key to successful teaching. The great teachers are never satisfied with their instruction; they are always looking to improve. This chapter will provide simple tools you can use to expand your teaching arsenal.

Appendix A: Differentiation Self-Assessment

A tool you can use to self-evaluate your current full-class instruction.

Appendix B: Overview of RTI

An overview of the full Response to Intervention process so you can put Tier One Full-Class Instruction in context.

Appendix C: Additional Reading and Resources

Let the learning continue with the list of great books and resources.

The goal of this book is to help you maximize your full-class instruction. It is designed to give you the tools necessary to meet the individual needs of your students each day. Use it alone, use it with colleagues, use it often. Make this the year that you decide to Maximize your Full-Class Instruction!

Pat Quinn
"The RTI Guy"
www.TotalRTI.com

Chapter One

FOUR DIRECTIONS

Students need direction. It is my experience that students rarely stand still. They're either moving in the right direction, or they're moving in the wrong direction. Your students need to be headed in the right direction. I believe there are four types of directions that students need, and all four need to be pointed in the same direction. I picture it like four wheels on a car. If all four wheels aren't headed in the right direction, the car isn't going to move very well. So let's look at the four directions that a student needs to be moving correctly.

Self- Direction

The first direction that students need is self-direction. Self-direction is a feeling of control—that they actually have some control over the outcome.

You have some control over your own destiny. A student needs to know that they have choices that they can make. Students also need to know that the teacher listens to their opinions and values their thoughts, feelings, and opinions. Teachers often get into control battles with students. There are some students who come into your classroom every day, not with the goal of learning, not with the goal of getting help. There are some students who come into your classroom every day with the goal of taking control of your classroom. As a teacher, if you engage in this battle with them, you will battle with them every day. With some students, the more you care, the less they act like they care. With others, the harder you push, the more they push back.

Mistakes teachers make in this area include being controlling and trying to control every aspect of a student's time with them. Group punishment and group rewards are other mistakes. Anytime you say to your class, "If one person misbehaves, the entire class is going to get punished," you steal control from the student and they feel powerless to affect their own outcome. Anytime you say to a student, "If everybody in class does this, then you will receive this reward," you steal power from students and they feel a lack of control.

Now I know many teachers will respond to this by saying, "Wait a minute, this works." It may work with 80% of your students, maybe 90% of your students. But with roughly 10% of your students, when you steal control, it drives them crazy. Those are the 10% that stop moving forward, stop being motivated, and stop engaging with you. Those are the 10% whose performance we're trying to improve. You might say, "This is working for me." And the data might show that for 80% of your students, group punishment, group rewards, and group grading does work. But if you're trying to improve the performance of the 10% you are in a control battle with, that is the wrong approach.

Instead, consider individual accountability as a hallmark in your classroom. Always talk to students about the fact that they control the outcome in your class. Each student determines whether they are successful or unsuccessful in their class—and the performance of another student doesn't change that.

Grading on a curve is another thing that teachers do that steals control away from students. The performance of one student in your class should not affect the grade of another student in your class. Grading students on group projects, if the student does not get to choose his own group, is another thing that teachers do that steals control from students. If you're going to place three students in my group who don't try, don't have background information, and have made poor decisions in the past and tell me that my grade is attached to their performance on this project, you have stolen my power, stolen my ability to control my own destiny, and stolen from me the very chance at success that I was hoping to have in this class. The teacher who does that has made a choice to design the grading policy so that I do not have control over my own grade. And when you do that, if you don't think you are hurting the motivation and engagement of certain students in your class, you just are not seeing the damage that you are doing.

Instead, make sure that students know they control their own destiny, their own grade, in your class. It is not affected by the performance of other students. Build choices into everything that you do in your class. Every time you give an assignment, students should have choices—choices of where to do the assignment, choices of when to turn it in, and perhaps choices of which of two assignments they do. You can give them choices of how they will complete a particular assignment. That doesn't mean you don't have parameters on your choices, guidelines for their choices, and certainly standards about standing performance when they do turn in an assignment. It does mean that you are allowing students to have a say in their future. You're allowing students to have some control in small ways.

But in this area of control, little ways of providing control make all the difference. I always tell teachers that the next time they give an assignment, instead of assigning 1 through 10, assign 1 through 12 and tell students they can skip any two items on the assignment. The next time you give a test or a quiz, tell students they can skip any one problem on the test or quiz and test anxiety will go down. Test performance will go up, and students will feel more relaxed, more comfortable, and more in control of their own destiny.

Giving the students a sense of self-direction in your class is one of the four big directions that every student needs to actively engage and be fully motivated to maximize tier one instruction.

Academic Direction

The second direction that every student in your class needs is academic direction, otherwise known as skills direction. This means that the student believes they have the skills, or the knowledge, necessary to be successful in your class. Every day, every student walks into your classroom and asks themselves a question. "If I try today, do I have a chance of being successful?" If they answer yes to that question, they will try. If they answer no to that question, they will not try. So, as a teacher, your job is to make sure students know that they have a chance at success today—that you will put them in a position with their current skills and current knowledge to be successful in class today.

Students need to know two things: First, that I can be successful today if I try. And second, that the teacher is on my side—that the teacher is not working against me or out to get me. Mistakes that teachers make in this area include showing happiness or delight when they catch students making mistakes, or gloating that they are smarter than students or able to catch students in simple errors. I have seen some teachers who mark problems wrong on a test or quiz in red with such delight and glee that the check mark covers the entire page. And when they write written comments, they put three exclamation points on it to show the student how wrong they were. Trust me, you're not showing any student that you are on their side when you do that.

I like to ask students, "Does you teacher want you to be successful?" You'd be surprised how many students answer "no" to that question. And when I asked them, "Why did you answer no to that question?," they say, "The teacher loves to catch me doing things wrong. The teacher loves to point out my mistakes. The teacher is simply not on my side."

To help students understand that they can be successful today, your lesson needs to be designed so that even a student who comes in lacking some prerequisite skills can be successful. This involves a level of differentiation and pre-teaching of prerequisite skills so that you can hopefully get students up to speed in an attempt to be successful on this given day. Sometimes it will also require differentiating today's assignment so that students can be successful.

I am not a big advocate of differentiating assessment at the end of a unit because I think it gives a false impression to students and parents about where they are performing in relationship to their peers and the standards. But I do think on a day-to-day basis, you can create experiences for the students in your classroom where they can feel that they are moving in the right direction toward academic success. I hope that you will create an environment in your classroom where even students who lack prerequisite skills and background knowledge, even students who learn at a slower rate than other students, can feel like they have a chance of being successful every day in your classroom That's academic direction or skills direction, and it will get students moving in the right direction.

Career Direction

The third direction that every student in your class needs before they can be successful and fully engaged with you in class is career direction or life direction. This involves making goals in regard to what they want to do after their current level of schooling. As students get older, this includes, "What school do you want to go to after high school? Do you want to go to college or technical school? What career do you think you want to end up in?" I think it is important for students at all grade levels to have a life plan and life goals and career goals. People often tell me that it's not important for a first grader to have life goals or career goals, and I strongly disagree. I have all first graders, second graders, and third graders tell me their life goals, their career goals. Will they change? Of course, they will—but so will the life and career goals of a 30 year old. The fact that their career goal or life goal is going to change over the next 12 years shouldn't stop you from asking your students, "What are your goals?"

I ask all my students to write down a one paragraph life plan, telling me what their life's going to look like. Some teachers draw out this assignment even more and have students write an autobiography starting from today and moving forward. Some teachers have their students write an obituary. "When you die at the ripe old age of 99 years old, what are people going to say about you? What were your greatest accomplishments? Tell me about your family, where you lived, what your career was? Tell me everything about your life, looking back on it after you die at the age of 99 years old." This is a great activity for students to ask, "What am I working toward? What do I really want in life?" Remember, the idea here is not that these plans won't change. Of course, they're going to change. The idea here is that students have goals.

When you ask students, "What is your goal in life? What is your career goal?" The worst possible answer is, "I don't know." This is the worst possible answer because a student without goals has real difficulty seeing the relevance of your curriculum. It is impossible to make your curriculum relevant to a student if they don't have goals. If you find you have a student who has no goals, no aspirations, or no career goals, you should take time to help them learn about their options and select one. Of course, it will change in the future. That's not the point. The point is that they're working toward something and now you can attach everything you do in your class to that goal.

One activity some teachers do to help develop students' goals and learn about their life aspirations is called, "Question of the Day." Question of the Day takes 6 minutes out of your class for 10 days in a row. For 10 days straight, I want you to begin class by asking your students a simple question (you will ask a different question each day). Based on the age level of your students, Question of the Day questions may include: "What are your hobbies? What do you like to do in your free time? Do you enjoy any sports?" For younger students, you may need to start with: "Do you have brothers and sisters? What's your favorite color? Tell me about your pets. Tell me about your family." Everybody should be asked questions like "What are your hopes? What are your dreams? What are your fears? What do you think you want to do in life after you get out of high school?" After you ask the question, give the students two minutes to write their answer, two minutes to share their answer with a friend, and two minutes if anybody wants to share their answer with the full group. This activity consumes 6 minutes a day for 10 days. In a school year, this takes one hour out of your full curriculum. I'm sure you can afford one hour to find out your students' goals, their hopes, their dreams, and their aspirations.

At the end of this process, you'll have 10 pieces of paper for each student that you can staple together in a little booklet. I'd love to tell you that I read every student's booklet every year, but I don't. Oftentimes, I throw them in my bottom filing cabinet drawer. But when I do struggle with a student, when I do find a student is wandering around directionless, I will often pull out their booklet, their 10 answers to the questions of the day, and read through it. It will make me better able to address the student's needs, talk to the student about his or her interests, and engage the student on a deeper level.

When other teachers at our school have come to me and said, "I'm struggling with a student that you have in class," I will often pull out their book and give it to them. I'll say, "I have a book about this student. Do you want to read it?" And they always say yes. Getting students to develop goals is an extremely important part of your job. You know how your curriculum relates to certain careers and certain schooling options after high school. It's important for you to talk to students about what their options are and how the decisions they make today will lead to their future.

When it comes to career direction, students need to know two things: "What do I want to do in the future?" and "How is this going to get me there?" Some teachers think that it's not important to connect their curriculum to real life or to their students' futures. But it is important. Every time you teach a new objective to your students, you should show them how it relates to their current life and to their life in the future. Without knowledge about your students' goals, you will not be able to do this adequately. But when you know your students' goals—their life goals, their career goals, their schooling goals—you are better able to connect what you are teaching now with what they're going to be doing in the future. If you find that you're teaching something that you cannot connect to their future, maybe you should evaluate whether or not it should actually be in your curriculum. If you find that you don't know how something you're teaching relates to their life now or in the future, maybe you should evaluate that portion of your curriculum or learn more about it so you are better able to connect it to your students' futures. Having direction in their career, having direction in life, is an important quality for students to actively engage and be motivated.

I've heard lots of teachers call students lazy, but I don't believe students are lazy. I believe they sometimes lack goals and aspirations. That's very different from lazy. Lazy is a quality you are attaching to the actual person. Not having goals and aspirations is a temporary situation that we can teach and repair. Rather than label a student "lazy," ask them what their goals and aspirations are, and if they have none, work toward solving that problem. Getting your students pointed in the right direction in their career and life is an important step to actively engaging your students.

Relationship Direction

The fourth direction that every student needs is relationship direction. Relationship direction can involve two things: Relationships with peers their own age, or friendships with students who are their own age, or a relationship with the adult in the classroom. Either one will do—you don't need both. A student either needs relationships with friends their own age in the classroom or a relationship with the teacher in the classroom. But if both are missing, the student can become isolated, separated, and start to disengage from the rest of the class.

A student needs to know two things: First, where do I fit in socially? And second, that I am safe when I am in this classroom. Maslow's Pyramid of Human Needs has been looked at for years as part of the educational structure of every classroom. Yet these days, it is often discarded as "old school" thinking. But the pyramid is still an important part of what students actually need in your classroom, and at the base of the pyramid are core needs such as safety. If students don't feel safe in your classroom, they cannot learn, they cannot engage, be motivated, concentrate, or receive new material and process new material.

The mistake teachers make in this area is simply to believe that relationships are not that important. I know some teachers who tell me, "I teach math, not relationships. I teach science, not relationships." They simply do not understand that unless students have relationships in their classroom, they are not going to learn at the same level that they would if they did have relationships. I know teachers who say, "My curriculum is crowded. I don't have time to build relationships. I don't have time to get to know my students." My answer is simple. You don't have time not to know your students. It takes much longer to engage a student, motivate a student, and get a student to learn if you do not have a relationship with them. On a daily basis, you have to convince those students to trust you and to trust that you're taking them to a good place. Contrast that to a student with whom you do have a good relationship, who trusts that you're taking them to a good place, and think of the time you will save. It's simply convincing students that you can be trusted every day.

An activity teachers can do to help build relationships with students is called "relationship checklist." To create a relationship checklist, take a list of the students in your class, and, across the top of the page, list facts that you want to know about your students. At the youngest grades, these facts may include their favorite color, how many brothers and sisters they have, or whether they have any pets. As students get older, it might be, "Do you have any hobbies? What do you like to do on weekends? Are there any sports that you enjoy?" For students nearing or in high school, it might be, "What do you want to do after high school? Do you want to go to college? Have you thought about which college you want to go to?" Then, over the course of the next month, when you know a fact about a student, put an "X" or a checkmark in that column under that fact. If you do this for one month, you'll find that you know everything about certain students. Maybe you had them in class last year, maybe you had their older brothers and sisters, maybe you're friends with their parents, but you know everything about them. What you will also find is that there are certain students who have very few checkmarks. You know little about them. Oftentimes, the students who have no checkmarks in one class at your school will have no checkmarks with any teachers in your school. These are the students who are falling through the cracks. You need to be intentional in your efforts to form better relationships with them. A student who has no peer relationships and no relationship with the teacher in the classroom is highly at-risk in your school and in your classroom. You need to focus your attention on this and get your students in a good relationship direction so that those students can fully engage and you can maximize tier one instruction.

The four directions that students need are self-direction, academic direction, career direction, and relationship direction. I know many teachers who think one or two of these are important, but let the others fall by the wayside. That is a mistake. Each of these four directions is extremely important. A student can have three of the four and they will struggle to engage and be motivated. Teachers will often label a student like that as "belligerent," "lazy," or "not very smart." But that is simply not the case. The student could be a student with very high potential but because they are missing one of these four directions, they have difficulty engaging and difficulty being motivated in class. It is easy for teachers to say, "This is not my problem to solve; that this is the student's problem. They need to figure this out." Or, "This is the guidance counselor's problem; they need to figure it out." Or my favorite, "This is the parents' problem; they need to work on this problem." In all of those answers, you are passing the buck to someone else. If you value your content, if you value your curriculum, if you believe that it's important for students to learn what you are teaching, then I would think you would want to do everything in your power to help them learn it. Helping students to move in the right direction in these four areas is what it takes to get students to learn your content. Helping students to get moving in the right direction in these four areas is doing everything you can to help students succeed and achieve in your classroom. It is the only way to maximize your full-class instruction.

Chapter Two

TEACHING
INDIVIDUAL DIFFERENCES

So, you have made the decision to break your class into two groups and do different activities with these two groups...or you have simply decided to individualize instruction within large group instruction. After you have made that decision, the next step you need to take is extremely important: You need to teach your students about their individual differences.

I can walk into a school and tell right away if this step has been skipped. Many teachers I know have tried differentiated instruction. They've tried differentiated instruction, as well. And when you do, you'll sometimes get resistance. Outstanding instruction requires that some students at your school get stuff that other students at your school don't get. Some students at your school get instruction, progress monitoring, and interventions—they get stuff that other students don't get. That's part of great instruction. And if you have not taught your students about their individual differences, the first time this happens, students are going to be looking around saying, "How come they're getting that and I'm getting this? How come they have that assignment and I have this assignment? How come you said that to them and not to me?" And then parents will start calling and saying, "What about this, what about that?" In my experiences, the moment a regular classroom teacher gets that resistance, they stop using differentiated instruction—they stop using the techniques they should be using. You will get that resistance if you skip this step. But if you do this step, you won't get that level of resistance. Teach your students about individual differences.

There are three specific areas that I want you to teach your students in regard to individual differences. The first is to teach them about their differences in background information. Some students come to you knowing an awful lot; some students come to you knowing an awful little. Every single time you, the teacher, walks into the classroom to teach something new to your students, some of the students sitting in front of you already know everything that you're going to say that day. It's also true that some of the students sitting in front of you don't know anything about what you're going to say that day. They may not even understand some of the words that you're going to use. That happens every single day.

The second area that I'd like you to teach your students about their individual differences is rates of learning, or how fast students learn. Some students learn new material quickly. Some students learn new material slowly. Some students learn new material the first time they're exposed to it. For other students, it takes multiple exposures to a piece of information before they learn something. As a matter of fact, 80% of you will find that 80% of your students require multiple exposures to a piece of information before they learn something. This makes, "I've already taught you that!"

or "How many times do I have to tell you?" the strangest thing a teacher can say. It's normal to take multiple exposures to a piece of information before a student will learn it.

The third area that I'd like you to teach your students about their individual differences is how students learn. You can call that multiple intelligences—you can call it learning style—there are a lot of names for it. But we know that some of our students learn best by listening, some of our students learn best by watching, and some of our students are kinesthetic learners. They learn best when they can physically participate in the learning.

There are activities that teachers can do to teach their students about these individual differences. I'd like to show you a few of them right now. On the first day of school every year, one teacher I know takes her class out of the classroom and to the gymnasium and says, "Line up here on the edge of the gymnasium, and in a moment, I'm going to give you two instructions. It's very important that you follow both instructions." The kids are so excited—it's the first day of school, they get to go down to the gym---for them, this is very exciting. She says, "The first instruction is when I say go, I want you to run across the gym as fast as you can. That's the first rule. You have to run as fast as you can." And the kids are so excited because they are going to get to run across the gym—this is going to be great. But then the teacher says, "There's a second instruction. The second instruction is that I want every student in class to get to the other side of the gym at the exact same time. You have to get there at the exact same time."

You know kids want to follow instructions—they really do—but these two instructions don't really make sense together. The students are all standing in a big line, and the first hand pops up in the air. The teacher calls on the little boy, who says, "That doesn't make any sense. If we all run as fast as we can, we're not all going to get to the other side of the gym at the exact same time." This is a great way to teach your students that even if they all try their hardest this school year, they are going to end up in different places, and they're going to get there at different times.

There's an activity I always do with my students on the second day of school. I get them all out of their desks and have them come up to the front of the classroom and line up in a straight line across the front of the classroom. When they're all lined up in a straight line across the front of the room with the door to the side, I tell them that their assignment is to take two steps and touch the door. Well, the kids who were standing right by the door are loving this class. It's only the second day of school, and they're thinking that they're already doing very well. They take one step, two steps, and they touch the door. The students that are standing a little further away say, "This is going to be tough, but I can take really big steps. I think I can do this." So they take one giant step, two giant steps, and they touch the door. But what about the students who are standing to the other side, too far to touch the door? What do they say? They say, "That's not fair." I say, "What do you mean that's not fair? I gave everybody the exact same assignment. Of course, that's fair." They say, "Well, it's not fair." I repeat, "Well, of course it's fair. I gave everyone the exact same assignment. Why wouldn't that be fair?" They answer, "Well, we're all starting at different spots."

Well, now we're talking. Now we're teaching, because when the students walked into this classroom, they were all starting in different spots. And so I'd say, "What would be fair?" And somebody will raise their hand and say, "Well, I think what would be fair is that the students who are standing over here should get two steps to touch the door, the students who were standing over there should get four steps to touch the door, and the students who were standing over there should get six steps to touch the door." And I say, "I think you're absolutely right. There will be times this school year when we have different steps to the same goal." The students can all have the same goal, but they will take different paths to it.

You shouldn't expect everyone in the school to have the same assignment every night. That wouldn't make any sense. We're all starting in different spots. And in five minutes, I've taught students two of the most important concepts I'll teach all year. In five minutes, I've taught two concepts that I'll refer back to dozens of times this school year. The first is that we all start in different spots. If that's the only thing this activity taught, it would be worth the five minutes it takes to do it. The second concept is that we all take different steps to the same goal. And I'll refer back to these two concepts dozens of times during the school year.

There is another activity, called Emergency Room, that I do on the third day of school. Emergency Room teaches one single concept. That concept is, "When everyone gets the exact same thing, it's not fair. Emergency Room is a game I play with students, as well as with parents. Any time I'm in front of parents, such as on parent night or during open house, I'll play Emergency Room. In this game, you pass out index cards that list medical problems. One person gets a card that says they have a sprained wrist. Another person gets a card that says they have a headache. Someone else gets a card that says they have a broken ankle, and another person's card says they have a bloody nose. When everyone has a card, I open up the emergency room at the front of the classroom. The first student or the first parent walks up and says, "I have a sprained wrist." And I wrap a bandage around their wrist. The next person comes up and says, "I have a headache." I wrap a bandage around their wrist and send them back to their desk. The next person comes up and says, "I have a broken ankle." And I say, "How'd you get up here?" Then I wrap a bandage around their wrist and they go back to their desk. The next person come up and says, "I have a bloody nose." And again, I wrap a bandage around their wrist and they go back to their desk. When everyone gets the exact same thing, that's not fair. What is fair is giving everyone what they need. It's an important concept to teach to your students and their parents.

Many teachers I know have tried differentiated instruction. When they do, they get resistance from students and their parents, so they stop. That's a clear sign that you haven't spent enough time teaching your students about their individual differences.

Here's another story that teaches students about individual differences. As a teacher, I walk into the classroom with a box that contains 25 pairs of size 7 shoes. About a month into the school year, I walk into class and dump the box out into the middle of the classroom and tell everybody to put on a pair of shoes. Some of the students find that the shoes fit like clown shoes. They're huge on them. For some of the students, they fit just perfectly. And it's painful to watch some of the students try to put their big feet into shoes which are obviously far too small. It doesn't take long and somebody says, "That's not fair." I say, "What do you mean it's not fair? I gave everyone the exact same thing." Again, they'll argue that it's not fair, but I won't back down. "Well, of course it's fair, I gave everybody the exact same thing. What would be more fair than that?" And they say, "Well, it would be more fair if we all got the size that we need." Well, now we're talking. Now we're teaching, because this school year, I'm not trying to give all of you the exact same pair of shoes. I'm trying to give all of you the pair of shoes that you need. Through activities like this, you can teach your students about their individual differences.

Some teachers use classroom roles to teach individual differences. Not assigned randomly, these classroom roles aren't rotated throughout the whole class. You will have students with unique characteristics, and you should choose roles for those students that meet their individual characteristics and their individual needs. I bet you have a student who has trouble staying in their desk, who's always out walking around the classroom. What would be a great role for that student? They could pass papers out for you. They could collect papers for you. They could run errands for you.

One year, I had a student who talked really loud. Have you ever had that student? It was like his voice was at 11 the whole time. Everybody hated him. The other students did not like him. I put him in a seat by the door, and I made him our classroom announcer. If somebody would show up at the door, he would pop out of his desk and stand up and say, "Ladies and Gentlemen, the principal!" He was one of the most popular students after I did that. Everybody loved him...and by the way, people loved stopping by our classroom—it was like being on the red carpet. They were introduced when they came to our classroom. About two weeks after that, another student came up to me and asked, "Can I be the classroom announcer?" My answer was "No. The role classroom announcer was given to that student because he had a unique characteristic. Now tell me what's unique about you, and we'll come up with a role for you." So everybody gets a role, but they aren't assigned randomly, and they certainly aren't rotated, because we're all different. Through the assignment of classroom roles, you can really help kids identify what's unique about themselves and each other.

Please don't skip this step. It is easy to rush into differentiated instruction, but that is a mistake. Doing so without teaching your students about their individual differences is a recipe for a class that rebels and objects.

Instead, start by spending some time teaching your students that their individual differences are normal and expected. Most importantly, teach your students that you are ready to help ALL students learn.

Chapter Three

SEVEN ESSENTIAL LESSON COMPONENTS

This chapter covers the seven components of good lesson design. Some people will say, "I learned the seven components of good lesson design my freshman year of college. Why are you covering this on maximizing full-class instruction?" The answer is simple. Even though most teachers include many of these seven components in every lesson, they often do not maximize the effectiveness of each component.

I believe you can approach this chapter in two ways. You can listen to each component and say, "I already do that. I'm going to stop listening." Or you can look at each component and say, "I can make that better in my classroom. I could maximize my instruction by improving each of the seven components." I hope you'll choose the second option and look at these seven components with an eye for improvement in every aspect of each of your lessons.

Essential Lesson Component 1: Attention

The first component of good lesson design is attention. You must direct and focus the students' attention on your instruction. Many teachers tell me they have difficulty getting their class to become quiet at the beginning of class. They often have trouble calming the class down, getting them to stop talking, and focusing their attention. Teachers will often tell me that they waste two or three minutes, sometimes up to five minutes, at the beginning of each class period just trying to get the class focused.

There are specific things you can do at the beginning of class to focus the attention of your class and get your students ready for instruction. Before the class begins, I like teachers to have three non-verbal cues that instruction is ready to start. Non-verbal cues do not include the teacher shouting from the front of the classroom. It doesn't involve yelling over the volume of the students. Non-verbal cues are things you can do that focus the attention of your students and let them know class is going to begin.

Some examples of non-verbal cues that teachers can use at the beginning of class include closing the door, and, by the way, don't be afraid to close the door loudly. It's a great non-verbal cue. Another example would be to blink the lights off and on. Some teachers stand in the same spot every time they begin instruction, so if you a theatric approach, go to that spot and step into that one space, and your students will know that you are ready to begin instruction. Other teachers turn on music, turn off music, or hold up two fingers to indicate they are ready to begin. It is time to be quiet and focus your attention on the teacher. Do you have three non-verbal cues that you use at the beginning of class to let the students know it is time for instruction to begin?

Once the students are quiet and ready for instruction, focus their attention on the upcoming lesson and increase their interest in what you are going to teach. You want to do this for two important reasons. The first goes back to one of our core concepts, which is the curriculum must be relevant for students to be ready to receive it. Your attention-getting device is a great opportunity for you to show the relevance of what you are teaching. You can connect the curriculum to your students' life goals or career goals. You can connect the curriculum to their personal interests. You can connect the curriculum to their past prior knowledge. All of these will increase the relevance of what you are trying to teach.

The second reason that you want to use an attention-getting device to raise interest and receptiveness of the students to the instruction you are about to deliver is that students are more open to receiving instruction when they believe it is going to be exciting and fun to learn. Choosing a good attention-getting device, choosing a good attention-getting demonstration, and choosing an activity at the beginning of class that will focus the attention of the class and make them ready to receive what you are trying to teach is an essential component of good lesson design. When evaluating any lesson that you deliver, start your evaluation at the very beginning. Did you use non-verbal cues to draw the attention of the class to you? Once you had their attention, did you use a good attention-getting device to increase the receptiveness of your students, increase their interest, and show them the relevance of today's objective?

Essential Lesson Component 2:
Pre-Assessment

The second component to good lesson design is pre-assessment. Before you begin instruction, it is extremely important that you are knowledgeable about your students' prior knowledge in the particular area that you're trying to teach. I can't tell you how many times I observe a lesson, and at the end of the lesson, I ask the teacher, "Do you think your students were ready for this lesson? Do you know which students had the prerequisite skills and which did not have the prerequisite skills to receive this lesson? Did you know ahead of time whether or not your students had the background information to perform well in this lesson?" Oftentimes, the answer is, "No." They do not have any knowledge about the background information or knowledge of their students, yet they go ahead and teach the lesson. Why? Because their curriculum says today's the day I'm supposed to teach this lesson. Even if you're being held to the tightest pacing guide, it will still benefit you to pre-assess the knowledge of your students before you begin instructing the lesson. It will change the way you instruct the lesson. This information is vital for you to maximize full-class instruction.

Your lesson should begin with you pre-assessing the skills and knowledge of your students in the particular area that you are going to address that day. This may take the form of a short pre-test. It may take the form of a quick game. It may take the form of a simple question and answer period with your students. In many classes, this is work that is done before the bell. Some teachers would call this bell work or board work. Whatever you call the activity that you do when students come to class, they begin it right away. It may be something you've written on the board or projected onto the screen prior to them even entering the room. It can become one of your class routines—when the students come in, they sit down and immediately begin working on this activity. That's a great way to pre-assess the knowledge of your students.

It also is a great classroom management technique because it focuses the student's attention on learning, rather than talking and goofing around. It also gives you a chance to take attendance, talk to particular students, and speak with the students who were absent yesterday and missed previous class instruction.

Begin your class with a pre-assessment of their prior skills or knowledge. Some teachers will do this at the end of class they day before, so they have this knowledge overnight as they plan instruction for the next day. That's a great way to use the knowledge you're going to gain from this pre-assessment to drive your instruction. Whichever way you do it, make sure you never begin instruction until you have a firm grasp on which students have the prerequisite skills, and which ones do not have the prerequisite skills, for the lesson that you are going to deliver today.

Essential Lesson Component 3:
Instruction

The third component of good lesson design is instruction. You may think it's silly to include instruction in a list of lesson design components. Who would deliver a lesson without instruction? However, I observe lessons all the time where the teacher completely skips over instruction. And certainly if instruction is included in a lesson, it is one of the areas where teachers fail to maximize the potential of any lesson. Don't skip instruction. Don't just evaluate or give feedback on yesterday's assignment and move right in to practicing today's new skill. At some point in the lesson, make sure you actually give instruction on the new content or new skill that you are expecting students to learn and apply. And when you do deliver instruction, make sure you maximize the potential of this part of your lesson. That is done by using research-based, best practice instructional methods for your subject area and grade level, and by differentiating instruction so that it is delivered at the correct level for as many students as possible in your classroom.

I would like teacher to focus on two things when they are giving instruction. The first is to connect what you're teaching today to the prior knowledge of the students. It is necessary to constantly remind students that you are not teaching an isolated skill that you just picked out of the sky, or that dropped into your lap one day. Instead, constantly show your students the overall fabric of the bigger picture. Show them that this little slice of knowledge, content, or skill that you're teaching them today does fit into the broader framework of your subject area and does fit into the bigger picture of what you want them to learn this school year and throughout the course of their life.

One of the best ways to do this is to connect what you're teaching today to your students' prior knowledge. This can be a shared common experience. This can be something you taught earlier in the school year. This can be something you know they learned earlier in their schooling life. Teachers who skip this step and teach today's objective as an isolated incident or as a stand-alone little blip on the screen often wonder why their knowledge doesn't transfer, why students don't learn the first time, and why students have trouble making connections to the larger picture. As a teacher, when you don't make connections to the larger picture, the relevance of what you're teaching goes way down, as does the students' motivation and receptiveness to learning. On the other hand, teachers who do connect every lesson to the prior knowledge of the students and where it fits in the bigger picture, find that their students are more motivated, more receptive to the learning, and retain more of the information because their mind has a place to file it, a place to put it. They have a place to say this is where this fits into the bigger picture.

The second thing I want you to remember to do during instruction is to point out the relevance of what you are teaching. Remember that when the students do not see the relevance of the day's objective, their motivational levels go down, their receptiveness to learning goes down, and their engagement levels in class go down.

This is why knowledge of your students' career goals, life goals, and background all become so important. People often discard the "get to know me" activities conducted at the beginning of the school year when students share things about their summer, their past, their family, and most importantly, about their goals, dreams, and aspirations in future life. Don't discard these as fluff activities, and certainly don't ever say that this is a waste of time or something you don't have time to do. You don't have time not to gain this valuable knowledge about your students, because without it, you cannot make your instruction relevant to the students. It is during the instructional portion of your class, when you're actually teaching them the new content and the new knowledge, that it is your responsibility as the teacher to connect this slice of knowledge, skills, or content to the bigger picture and to the goals, aspirations, and dreams of your students.

Skip this step at your own peril. I've heard many a teacher complain that their students just are not retaining information, are not paying attention, and are not engaging. They make plenty of excuses. They tell me their students are lazy, unmotivated, don't have work ethics, and their parents aren't involved. But the real problem is that they did not take the time to learn about the goals and aspirations of their students and connect what they were teaching to those goals and those future plans of the students. You can say that's not your job, but if teaching your content, your curriculum, and your subject is your job, this is the way to do it. Connect the curriculum to your students' goals, aspirations, and dreams. That is how you maximize instruction in your classroom.

Essential Lesson Component 4:
Checking for Understanding

The fourth step of good lesson design is checking for understanding. After you have instructed your students for a period of time, it is important that you check for understanding. When I speak at seminars, I will often have the teachers in the room raise their hands if they have ever asked their students, "Are there any questions?" If you have asked your students that question, you have used the single, *least* effective check for understanding that has ever been invented. The very students who have questions in your class are often afraid to ask them. It's also true that the very students who have questions often don't know what a good question would even sound like. If I were speaking to you completely in French, and I asked you to ask a question only in French and you didn't know French, you'd have a very difficult time asking a good question. The same is true in math, science, and other academic languages that we speak. In many cases, students don't even know how to phrase or ask a good question.

Your check for understanding should have two characteristics. First, your check for understanding should include individual accountability. Teachers use many methods for checking for understanding. Some teachers ask a question and count how many hands go up. Some teachers ask a question and call on one person, and if they get it right, they believe that the class understands it. If that one student gets it wrong, they believe that the class does not understand it. Some teachers will ask, "Are there any questions, or does anybody need me to do another example?" None of these methods give you the data that you want. You want to know exactly which students understand what you have just taught and which students do not understand what you have just taught, because you are about to make one of the most important educational decisions you'll make every day: "Should I move on or should I go back and re-teach?" You need good data to make this decision. That is why I want your check for understanding to have individual accountability. Oftentimes, teachers will have a student work on a particular problem, respond to a particular writing prompt, or individually show that they understand the material that was just taught.

The second characteristic that I want to describe your check for understanding is I want it to be active, not passive. A passive check for understanding is to say, "Please raise your hand if you don't understand this." To me, that is like saying to the students, "Please raise your hand if you feel stupid. Please raise your hand if you want to be embarrassed in front of your peers. Please raise your hand if you want to be the one that slows down the entire class." That is why very few students raise their hands when you ask a question in this way. Now it's possible that teachers ask the question this way because they don't want to stop or slow down instruction. Let's face it, answering student questions does slow down your class. Answering student questions sometimes prevents you from completing your lesson. Answering student questions can knock you off your pacing guide. But answering student questions and checking for understanding is one of the most important things you do as a teacher. Please don't use a passive check for understanding just so you can keep rolling through your material.

You want your check for understanding to be active. You want students to actively show you that they understand the new knowledge or content that you have just taught. And you want individual accountability. So design your check for understanding so that students actively have to show you, one-on-one, that they know how to do this. If you use this type of check for understanding, when it is finished, you will be able to say definitively, "Out of my 25 students, 13 of them know how to do this, and 12 of them do not." Not only will you have that knowledge, but you will also know exactly which students do not know how to do what you have just taught and which students do understand today's objective. That knowledge is essential when making the decision to move on or to go back and re-teach. It is also essential if you are going to split your class into different groups for guided practice or any of the other steps.

Do not skip checking for understanding. There are many teachers who deliver instruction and move right into practice without ever asking the question, "Did the students actually learn what I was trying to teach?" Don't ever confuse teaching and learning, and don't ever confuse covering material with students learning new material. The only way you can say definitively, "I know that a certain percentage of my students actually learned what I taught today," is to have a solid check for understanding built into your lesson. It's one of the ways you can maximize instruction.

Essential Lesson Component 5: Guided Practice

The fifth component of good lesson design is guided practice. Guided practice is when you have students practice the new skill or practice the new content that you are trying to get them to acquire in a very supervised situation with a very short feedback time. The difference between guided practice and independent practice, which will come next, is the feedback loop and the amount of assistance you provide. The feedback loop in guided practice must be very short, usually less than two or three minutes. The students will attempt something and immediately know if they did it correctly or incorrectly and what they need to change to do it better.

In independent practice, the feedback loop is much longer. Often, they turn in the assignment one day and receive it back the next, or it might take even longer than that for them to get feedback on their performance. The other difference between guided practice and independent practice is the amount of assistance they receive. During guided practice, you are there to help them every step of the way. Often, their new skills and tasks have been broken down into very simple steps that you will work on, one at a time. In independent practice, you provide much less assistance, although you are always there to help the students, and the skills are not always broken down into as many sub-skills or smaller steps. The same is true with content. When learning new content, guided practice will have a very short feedback loop, and the content will be broken down into small bits. During independent practice, the feedback loop will be longer, and the content will be expected to be learned in larger blocks and given back to you in larger blocks — sometimes even assimilated with other pieces of information. So guided practice is an important part of every lesson, and you should never begin independent practice until students have had an opportunity with guided practice.

I want you to have four goals for all your guided practice activities. The first goal is feedback, which is probably the most important reason that we use guided practice activities. It is an opportunity for students to receive very fast feedback so that they can improve their performance. The more often you give students feedback on how they could improve their performance, the faster they improve. This is why teachers who skip guided practice find that their students improve slower than teachers who include this in every lesson. In a guided practice situation, you may be able to give a student feedback 10 times in 10 or 20 minutes. If you do that, the level of improvement will go up so much faster than if you just give them an assignment that is due tomorrow and only give them feedback once. Picture the difference when a student receives feedback and ways he or she can improve ten times, versus receiving that feedback only once. You can see why guided practice improves student performance so much faster if you include it in your lessons.

The second reason that you should do guided practice is that it gives you an opportunity to teach more. Oftentimes, it is during guided practice that you will realize that you left out some instruction, rushed through some instruction, or simply did not deliver one component of your instruction clearly enough. You'll realize this because the same mistakes will begin to pop up during guided practice. This gives you an opportunity to teach to the full class, a small group, or to an individual an additional piece of instruction that will help them overcome those obstacles. Delivering extra instruction is one of the important goals of guided practice.

The third purpose of guided practice is to determine if the independent practice assignment you are about to assign is appropriate for your students. In a perfect world, every student would receive their own individualized, personalized independent practice assignment. But, in reality, no teacher can give a class of 30 students 30 different assignments. That is very difficult. However, I do think it is manageable to give your class two different assignments. I think it's even manageable to give your class three different assignments, based on their readiness, background information, grade of learning, and learning style.

It is during guided practice that you determine, regardless of how many assignments you have available to you, whether or not it is appropriate for the students in your group or classroom. Look at their responses to guided practice and ask yourself these very important questions: "Is this assignment appropriate? Are they ready for it?" And, if you have multiple assignments available for you, perhaps a core assignment, an extension assignment, and a remedial assignment, ask, "Which of these three assignments should I assign to each particular student?" That is one of the big purposes of guided practice.

The fourth purpose of guided practice is to determine if the class is ready for independent practice. There have been many times when I have delivered a lesson to my class, and during guided practice, I realized they simply were not ready for independent practice yet. If you realize that during guided practice, do not, I repeat, do not assign the independent practice assignment. Nothing ruins the spirit, the motivation, and the engagement of your class faster than assigning an independent practice assignment that they are not ready for. It is frustrating, it's depressing, and it hurts motivation. It will also lower the level of student engagement tomorrow and every day thereafter if you give them an independent practice assignment that you have not fully prepared them for. I would rather you simply stop class and say, "We're not going to have an assignment tonight. I'm just going to teach you some more right now." Or stop class completely and say, "This broke down; let's try this again tomorrow." That would be a better use of your time, because you're not doing damage to your class by assigning an independent practice assignment that your students are not ready to complete.

If you can accomplish all four of these purposes with your guided practice activity, then you are maximizing the potential of this lesson through guided practice.

HOMEWORK

A word about homework... We are getting ready to discuss the independent practice portion of your lesson. Before we do, I just want to say a word or two about homework.

Teachers assign homework for many of the wrong reasons. Some teachers assign homework to fill the remaining time left in class so that students do not misbehave, create a lot of noise, or leave their desks during the remaining time left in class. Some teachers assign homework because they mistakenly think it adds rigor to their class. I can assure you that I know of very rigorous classes where the teacher never assigns homework, and I know classes where there are long homework assignments every night and the class is not rigorous. The amount of homework and the length of the assignment do not determine whether or not your class is rigorous.

Some teachers assign homework because parents expect it. That's not a good reason to assign homework, either. Some teachers simply assign homework because they gave that homework assignment last year and they haven't taken the time to think about the value or purpose of it. These are not good reasons to assign homework.

There is no research that shows that more homework creates better results. And in most classes, homework is not assigned for the correct reason.

The other problem with homework is that it is inherently discriminatory. Homework discriminates against students whose parents are not actively involved in the educational process. Two different students in your class will receive the exact same homework assignment. One of them will go home and struggle with it, and their parent is right there to help them and provide them with additional support and instruction. The other student goes home and struggles with the assignment, and their parent is nowhere to be found. These two students have a completely different homework experience based solely on the involvement of their parents, the background knowledge of their parents, and the willingness of their parents to actively participate in the educational process.

To me, the only reason to assign homework is if you are creating an experience that cannot be replicated in the classroom. Wouldn't it be much fairer to assign an assignment in class so that all of the students have the support of the teacher if and when they struggle? In that case, all students will have the availability of extra help and extra instruction when they struggle. A class that is designed like that is less discriminatory and more equitable to all students in the classroom.

The only reason to assign homework assignments is if you have an experience that cannot be replicated in the class. I'm not telling you never to assign homework. What I am telling you is that before you ever give a homework assignment, ask yourself, "Is there a way to replicate this experience in the classroom?"

There are times when you will answer that question with a "no." Sometimes the students have to do something at home, like accessing resources, interviewing a person at home, or looking at something outside. In that case, you will say, "No, you have to do a portion of this at home." There are other times when you're teaching advanced classes, when the amount of time it would take to complete the assignment would simply steal too much instructional time from the classroom. So you have to assign it as homework. But almost 80% of all homework assignments that are assigned could easily be replicated in the classroom with the equitable support of the classroom teacher offering the same help to every student. The teacher simply chooses to assign it as homework because parents expect it or they feel that it will be more rigorous, for all the wrong reasons.

Again, every time you give a homework assignment, ask yourself, "Is there an experience I can give the students in class that would teach the same thing or replicate the same outcome as this homework assignment?" Most of the time you will answer "Yes" to that question and not assign the homework.

Essential Lesson Component 6:
Independent Practice

The sixth component of good lesson design is independent practice. The goal for your independent practice assignment is to make it as short as possible, but long enough that the students still acquire the new skill or learn the new content. You want it to be as short as it can possibly be, but still accomplish your goal. This is a good guiding principle when determining the length of any assignment. The length of your independent practice assignment should not be affected by the amount of time left in class, and should not be affected by parent expectations or other factors. It should be as short as possible to accomplish your goal, which is to have the students acquire the new skill or learn the new content.

It is important that the independent practice assignment be at the correct level—targeted to the level of the student. Giving an independent practice assignment that is too difficult because the student does not have the background information, knowledge, or skills to complete correctly, is a recipe for a frustrated student who lacks motivation and engages less with you in the classroom. Giving an independent practice assignment that is too easy for your students is a recipe for misbehavior and students who are bored and engage less with you in the classroom. If teachers complain that their students are lazy, that their students won't engage, or that their students lack work ethic, oftentimes, the problem is that the assignments are being delivered at the wrong level. Therefore, make sure you are targeting the independent practice assignment to the correct level, which is the very level in which your students are currently working.

Finally, independent practice assignments should include opportunities for students to check to see if they are completing the assignment correctly. You are not doing anyone a favor by having students work for 45 minutes or an hour on an assignment, only to find out that they were doing the wrong assignment, doing the assignment incorrectly, or not following the directions completely. So build in to every assignment an opportunity for your students to check to see if they are doing it correctly during the process of completing the independent assignment.

The best independent practice assignments are completed in class, where all students have an equal opportunity to get help from the teacher and other instructional resources. If you find that a low percentage of your students are completing your independent practice assignment, you can look at a number of common errors to determine the reason. Was the assignment too difficult for the students? Were the students not ready for independent practice, and you should have spent more time in guided practice? Or was the assignment too easy for the students? Other common errors include not giving students an opportunity to check as they go and not giving students the extra help or instructional support that they need during the completion of the independent practice assignment. Used correctly, independent practice is one way you can maximize the instruction in your classroom.

Essential Lesson Component 7:
Feedback

The seventh and final component of good lesson design is feedback. Now, don't ever confuse feedback with grading. I always tell teachers that they only have a certain number of minutes in their day, and if they picture their entire day as a giant pie, they want the section of their pie that is spent grading to be as small as possible. Grading doesn't help students very much at all. Grading is sorting students into different categories, and it isn't very beneficial for students. Feedback, on the other hand, is extremely beneficial for students. The problem with grading is that it's terrible feedback. If the only feedback you are giving your students is grading, you need to improve your feedback. I want the portion of your pie, the number of minutes you spend each day giving feedback to students, to be as large as possible.

Feedback is one of the most effective uses of your time as a teacher. When you're evaluating student work, keep this simple idea in mind: More feedback—less grading. The feedback that you give to your students should be fast and efficient. You should never give more time giving feedback on a particular assignment than it took the student to complete the assignment.

One of the ways you can make the feedback you give to students more efficient and effective is to shorten your assignments. This was discussed in the earlier section on independent practice. You want your independent practice assignments to be as short as possible, as long as they still accomplish your goal of having the students learn the new skill or acquire the new knowledge about the content. Teachers who give lengthy assignments often complain that they take a long time to grade. My response is always the same—give shorter assignments. It is a more valuable use of your time and the students' time.

Make sure your assignments are designed so you can quickly give feedback to students. If students turn in an assignment on Monday, and you don't give them feedback on their performance until Friday, it really is too long of a feedback cycle. The worst mistake you can make as a teacher is to have assignments due before a test, and not giving students feedback on that assignment until after the test. In that case, you have wasted the students' time, and you have wasted your time. The purpose of feedback is to improve performance. If you don't give the students feedback until after the test, you haven't improved their performance. Take a look at your lesson and unit design. If you often have an assignment due right before the test, but give the students feedback after the test, stop wasting everyone's time. Your goal is to spend as little time on grading as possible, so feel comfortable giving feedback to students without actually grading. Students will appreciate this, and you'll appreciate it because you will save time and energy for the most valuable process that you do, which is feedback.

I love Rubrics because Rubrics give great feedback. Rubrics actually show students, before they complete the assignment, how they are going to be evaluated and what good work actually looks like. Along with Rubrics, another great tool that teachers use are checklists. Checklists are lists of things you would like included in a well-done assignment. Before a student turns in their assignment, they can go through the checklist. A simple checklist might include, "Is your name on the paper? Did you use complete sentences? Did you answer the questions completely? Is your paper neat? Did you stay within the margins?" From there, you can include additional items in the checklist that are specific to that particular assignment. The quality of the work that students turn in will go up if you give them the checklist or the Rubric at the same time that you give them the assignment. If you give them the checklist or the Rubric after they turn in the assignment, or when they turn in the assignment, you aren't improving the quality of student work. The quality of student work improves when you give them the Rubric or the checklist *ahead* of time. So take the extra time and create a Rubric or a checklist for each of your assignments and watch how student work improves.

Shorten your feedback cycle to as little time as possible. It is best to give feedback immediately when the student turns in the assignment. Sometimes you can make that happen. The longest the feedback cycle should be on a typical assignment would be 24 hours. For instance, the student turns in the assignment one day, and the teacher provides the feedback the next day. If that seems impossible, there are two things you can do—you may need to adjust how you give feedback to your students, or you may need to shorten the assignment. Again, if students are turning in assignments and not receiving feedback for a week, or if they are receiving feedback after the summative evaluation or the end of unit or chapter test, there was no purpose to the assignment in the first place. The reason we give students assignments is so we can give them feedback and improve their performance. If you don't have feedback built into the process, then you were wasting your time. Used correctly, feedback can be one of the greatest tools you have to improve student performance and learning. Used correctly, the more often you give feedback, the faster your students will improve. This is why guided practice is an important lesson component and why feedback, after independent practice, is one of the ways that you can maximize the effectiveness of your instruction.

Essential Lesson Components: Putting It All Together

The seven components of good lesson design work together to create an atmosphere where all students can learn. It's a process that works from beginning to end, from the moment that class begins and you draw students' attention to your instruction, and onward to assessing if they are ready for instruction, the delivery of instruction and checking for understanding, multiple times during and after instruction. Guided practice begins the feedback loop. The more often you give feedback, the faster student performance will improve. Independent practice should be kept short and assessed quickly, and feedback should be given as soon as possible to continue the improvement cycle.

Remember, the seven components of lesson design do not have to happen within the confines of one day or one class period. Oftentimes, the class may begin with feedback on yesterday's independent practice, and then move into the attention and pre-assessment devices for today's lesson. Sometimes this seven-step process will take two full class days. In certain situations, it could take three days or a week. In certain cases, the cycle may be gone through twice in one class period. For those reasons, please don't feel restricted to do all seven steps on a particular day and don't be limited by doing the seven steps only once on a particular day. However, to maximize instruction in your classroom, do make sure your lessons include all seven of these components.

Chapter Four

OPPORTUNITIES TO
MAXIMIZE INSTRUCTION

I hate the term "differentiated instruction." I hate the term because it scares teachers. I hate the term because its meaning has become so confused over the years that teachers don't know what we ask, or expect, of them. I hate the term differentiated instruction because it is frustrating for teachers who are asked to do something, but the people who are asking them to do it don't even know what they're talking about.

Over the years, differentiated instruction has been misused to refer to a variety of activities that have nothing to do with true differentiation. From this point forward, I am not going to refer to these teaching strategies as differentiated instruction. Instead, I prefer to call them "opportunities to maximize instruction." I think this better describes what we are doing when we differentiate our lessons. Let's look at five different opportunities you have during every lesson to maximize your instruction.

Opportunity #1:
Pre-Assessment

The first opportunity that you have in each lesson to maximize your instruction happens during the pre-assessment component of your lesson. During pre-assessment, it is likely that you will find that some of the students in your class are ready for today's lesson, and some of the students in your class are not ready for today's lesson. This is a challenge, but every challenge becomes an opportunity. You have an opportunity at this point, early in your lesson, to level the playing field a little bit. You have the opportunity to take the students who lack the prerequisite skills that are necessary to be successful in today's lesson and help them quickly acquire some of those key prerequisite skills.

How do you do this? It involves splitting your class. It involves acknowledging to some students that they are ready for today's lesson, but because not everybody is, you need to take five minutes to level the playing field. It involves saying to other students in your class, "We're going to start today's lesson in a few minutes, but before we do, there's something I need to teach you." As a teacher, you need to become comfortable dividing your class into two groups. If you are not comfortable doing one activity with one group of students and another activity with a different group of students, you are not ready to maximize instruction in your classroom.

When you are ready to divide your class into two groups, here is a great way to do it. After the pre-assessment, take the students who are not ready yet for today's lesson and say, "We're going to begin instruction in a few minutes, but there are a few things I need to teach you first, so pay attention." Then spend a few minutes teaching them the prerequisite skills that are necessary. Not everything that the student is missing can be taught in this five minute period, but, hopefully, you'll be able to deliver a few key prerequisite skills or reminders of the background knowledge they already have that will help them to be successful in today's lesson.

At this point, there are two comments I should make. The first is that you are not trying to address every skill deficiency that every student has in your class. Certainly, you have students in your class who are lacking so many skills that it would take you five years to get them up to grade level, and certainly you have other students in your class who are lacking skills in many different areas. Don't try to remediate them all. Choose one or two essential skills that will help students be successful today. Choose the most essential skills that you can determine will create success for students today. Those are the one or two skills you want to focus on.

The second thing is that you will never level the playing field completely. When you walked into class, you had some students operating at a high level and some students operating at a lower level. In a perfect world, with a few minutes of remediation, everybody would be on the same level—but that is not going to happen. Your goal is not to completely level the playing field. Your goal is simply to tip the balance a little bit more toward success. This is why we don't spend 45 minutes on this remediation. It's why we're not even going to spend 20 minutes on this remediation. You get five minutes—five minutes while you let the students who are ready for today's lesson relax, work on something else, get started, read, prepare, or tutor another student, and five minutes for you to offer remediated instruction to other students in order to level the playing field a little and make the gap in your class a little smaller. Don't try to remediate all missing skills, and don't think that you're going to make your class a completely level playing field. The goal is just to tip it in your favor more than it was when the students walked in the door.

Teachers who do this—who stop before instruction begins and ask, "Can I level the playing field with some fast targeted instruction?"—maximize the effectiveness of their lessons because the lesson is now working with more students. Think of a typical class. When your students walk in, your core lesson is probably appropriate for about 50% of your class. For 25%, they already know everything you're going to say. They're way beyond what you'll teach today. Another 25% of your class is way below what you're going to teach today. They lack the prerequisite skills. Out of those 25%, what if you could take half or even 80% of them and get them ready for today's lesson? Automatically, you take a lesson that was going to be perfect for 50% of your class and appropriate for 75% of your class, and make it work for 87% or even 90% of your class. That is a nice improvement from five minutes of remediated instruction. So your first opportunity to maximize instruction in your classroom happens right after pre-assessment, when you ask, "Is everybody ready? And if they're not, is there something I could quickly teach them to level the playing field?"

Opportunity #2:
Check for Understanding

Your second opportunity to maximize instruction during your lesson happens during the check for understanding. Remember the check for understanding that you are going to do is going to have individual accountability built into it. You are not simply going to have students raise their hands if they understand. You're not just going to judge by the number of questions they might ask, and you're not going to ask, "Are there any questions?" Instead, you are going to give the students a chance to actively show you that they understand today's objective. Some of them will be able to do this in your check for understanding, and others will not. This is your second opportunity to maximize instruction.

If you have students who do not understand your initial instruction, it is an opportunity to break your class into two groups. Remember, to maximize instruction, you can't have your entire class always doing the same activity at the same time. In this situation, split your class into two groups. The group of students who understand today's objective as demonstrated in the active individual check for understanding can begin guided practice. Other students will receive more instruction. At some point during your check for understanding, you're going to break your class into two groups.

To one group, you can say, "You understand today's objective. You have actively shown me that with individual accountability. I'm going to let you begin guided practice. Here you go." To the other group, you're going to say, "At this point, you do not yet understand today's objective, and you are not ready for guided practice yet. I'm going to continue to teach you while the other students begin guided practice." Now of course, the goal of guided practice is that you're there to give feedback for students. You do not have a big block of instructional time here. Again, I want you to limit yourself to five minutes. Every time you maximize learning opportunities in your classroom, every time you maximize instruction, you can do it with five minute blocks of additional instruction. People who don't think five minutes will make a difference haven't sat in many classrooms. Five minutes of instruction can change everything. Five minutes of instruction can take a student who's not ready for a lesson and make them ready. Five minutes of instruction can take a student who's not ready for guided practice and make them ready for guided practice. Five minutes of instruction can increase confidence, competence, and a student's ability to accurately and correctly complete assignments. You can do all of that in just five minutes of instruction.

After breaking your class into two groups, one group will begin guided practice. In just five minutes, you're going to start giving them feedback on their work. The other group will be receiving additional instruction. When they show you that they do understand today's objective, they can begin guided practice immediately. During this five minute period, there may be multiple opportunities for them to show you that they are ready for guided practice.

This is your second opportunity to maximize instruction. You might not build this into every lesson. Remember, all five of these opportunities to maximize instruction do not need to be built into every lesson—but this is a great place to build in a break in your class. Divide your class into two groups, and maximize the learning in your classroom by giving additional instruction to specific students before guided practice.

Opportunity #3:
End of Guided Practice

The third opportunity to maximize instruction in your class happens at the end of guided practice. At this point, you will ask a question, and the answer will determine one of three options available to you. That question is, "Are they ready for independent practice, and is my independent practice assignment appropriate?" This gives you three options. You can answer the question, "Yes, they are ready for independent practice, and my assignment is appropriate." Doing so will allow you to give them an appropriate independent practice assignment, and they can get started as quickly as possible.

The second option is that you will determine that they are ready for independent practice, but today's assignment is not appropriate for them, so you will need a remedial assignment—or if the assignment is too easy for them, an extension assignment that applies the learning in a new situation or extends the learning in a new direction. Some teachers worry that this creates a lot of extra work, and it's true—good teaching is harder than bad teaching. However, I do not believe that it is an overwhelming amount of work to create two extra assignments once a week or once every other week in your classroom. Remember, you do not have to take advantage of all five of these opportunities to maximize instruction every day. Instead, pick and choose which lessons would be appropriate for these opportunities and slide them into your lesson plans on those particular days.

In addition to your core assignment, you may need a remedial assignment for those students for whom today's objective was too difficult, and an extension assignment for the students for whom the objective was too easy. You do not have to create these assignments since every major publishing company in the country includes, with every lesson in their curriculum, a remedial assignment and an extension assignment. But if you don't want to use the assignments that your publishing company has provided, you will have to create these assignments on your own. Give different assignments to different students in class. By that, I don't mean that you should have 30 different assignments for 30 different students. I mean you should have two assignments—one for those students who are ahead, and one for your students who are behind—or three assignments, one for students who are ahead of the objective, one for students who are right at the objective, and one for students who lack the prerequisite skills for today's assignment. This is far more manageable than creating a different assignment for each student.

Your third option is to answer the question, "Are my students ready for independent practice?" with, "No, they are not. They are just not ready for an assignment at this point, and I'm going to deliver more instruction." With those students, you would not assign independent practice, and you would use the remaining class time to deliver more instruction. Students learn at different rates, which means different students will need less or more minutes of instruction. In most classes, the fastest learner and the slowest learner receive the same number of minutes of instruction. On certain days, I hope you will give some students a chance to do independent practice and receive less instruction, and other students will actually skip independent practice and use all of the minutes that you have for instruction. This is one of the ways you can accommodate students who learn at different rates in your classroom, and it's your third opportunity to maximize instruction in your class.

At the end of guided practice, ask the question, "Are they ready for an assignment, and is this the appropriate assignment?" Then, choose from the three options. Some students will be ready. Some students will need the assignment adjusted up or down, and some students will not receive an assignment—they will simply receive more instruction. Use your options wisely, and you will maximize instruction in your classroom.

Opportunity #4:
Independent Practice

The fourth opportunity to maximize instruction in your classroom occurs during independent practice. In the previous opportunity, we talked about your chance to differentiate practice or give different students different independent practice assignments. In one class, some students may be working on the core assignment, while other students for whom today's objective was too easy are working on an extension activity. Different students in the same classroom may be working on a remedial assignment if you found that the objective was too difficult for them or they lacked the prerequisite skills to successfully complete today's independent practice. Along with differentiating the practice that you give them, or giving different students different assignments in your class, you can also check the students' work as they complete the independent practice. Remember, in the best lessons, independent practice is completed in class so students have an equitable opportunity to receive the extra help and instructional support that the teacher and the school provide.

As the students are completing the independent practice, implement the "check as you go" strategy. What does that mean? That means as they complete the assignment, there are certain points where they check to see if they are doing it correctly. One way to do that is to break a typical assignment into thirds. After the student completes 1/3 of the assignment, give them an opportunity to check and see if they are completing it correctly. That opportunity might include receiving feedback from the teacher, or checking their answers again an answer key, or consulting with another student or other resource that can give accurate and timely feedback to the student.

What does this accomplish? First, it ensures that students will not complete an entire assignment incorrectly. Second, students will not complete the wrong assignment. Third, students will not complete the assignment with incorrect instructions or incomplete instructions. Oftentimes, you can catch simple errors that the student is making again and again during this first check as you go. Often, students will be able to find their own errors and save a lot of time by building in a simple check as you go.

This is also an opportunity for you to adjust the assignment. If you find that the assignment is too difficult, you can shorten, adjust, change, or remove it. If you find the assignment is too easy, you can skip certain items and add others, or you can throw away the assignment completely and change the assignment. There are many ways that you can adjust the assignment to make it more appropriate if you check as you go.

Teachers who don't provide a check as you go opportunity during independent practice assignments find that certain students do a lot of work and then become very frustrated because they were doing the entire assignment wrong. Certain students might complete a lot of work and become very frustrated because they were doing the wrong assignment or had read the instructions and were doing the assignment in an incomplete or an incorrect way. Build in a simple check as you go to avoid these problems, shorten the feedback loop, and give yourself an opportunity to adjust the assignment, if necessary, to make it more appropriate for each student. This is your fourth opportunity in one lesson to maximize the instruction in your classroom.

Opportunity #5:
Feedback

The fifth and final opportunity to maximize instruction during your lesson occurs during the feedback or final component of your lesson. It is at this point that you evaluate the work the student has done on the independent practice assignment and give feedback. Remember, we want our feedback loop to be as short as possible. In the best case scenario, students would receive feedback the same day that they complete the assignment. At the very least, give them feedback the next day, no more than 24 hours after they have completed the assignment. We want to avoid a lapse of more than a week between the assignment being turned in and the student receiving feedback. We want to avoid giving feedback on the independent practice assignment after the summative assessment, the chapter test, or the unit test. And we want to avoid using grading as feedback because grading is terrible feedback.

The best feedback tells students what they're doing right, what they're doing wrong, and what they need to differently to do better next time. Grading doesn't do that. Grading simply categorizes students into one of five categories. Your feedback needs to be more specific than a letter grade or a percentage number. What is the student doing right? What is the student doing wrong? What does the student need to do differently to do better next time?

It is at this point during the feedback cycle, after independent practice, that you can make an important decision about your students. Did they understand the objective and correctly perform it for you? Did they learn the content, acquire the skill, or achieve the objective in your classroom? If you answer yes to that question, you can move on to the next lesson. But if you answered no, it is time to go back and re-teach. Don't move on to the next lesson if most of your class hasn't acquired the knowledge or skill in today's lesson. You can argue that you've got a pacing guide or an assessment coming up that requires you to move on, but, trust me, if most of your students didn't understand yesterday's lesson, they're not going to understand today's lesson. Don't move on. Go back and re-teach.

A difficult situation happens when half of your class understood yesterday's lesson and half of your class did not. As a teacher, that leaves you in a dilemma. This is why I recommend re-teaching some of your students at the start of the next lesson. Your first opportunity to maximize instruction involved breaking your class into two groups after the pre-assessment. You can do the same thing now. You can break your class into two groups. Start class the next day and say, "Based on how you did on independent practice, I see that some of you understand this, and some of you do not. Before we begin the next lesson, I'm going to re-teach for a short period of time." Remember, just five minutes of instruction can change everything. By re-teaching for a short period of time, you are helping to level the playing field once again. This extra five minutes after independent practice gives you an opportunity to help the students who didn't understand yesterday's lesson and give them some extra help with what they misunderstood or did not learn. This will give them a much better chance to be successful in today's lesson.

Of course, you don't have to do this. You could just plow forward into today's lesson knowing that a portion of your class is simply not ready for it and didn't even understand what they were supposed to learn yesterday. However, I think it is a much wiser instructional choice to spend a few minutes at the beginning of the next lesson helping the students who didn't understand the previous lesson and get them up to speed, so that everybody can benefit from today's lesson.

Remember our two rules when it comes to maximizing instruction: First you are never going to compensate for all of the prerequisite skills that a student lacks in this five minutes of re-teaching. You shouldn't try. You shouldn't try to cover up all of their weaknesses, fill in all the gaps, or teach them all of the skills that they lack. Instead, focus specifically on what they missed yesterday or what they need for today's lesson.

Second, even with re-teaching, you might not be able to bring every student up to the level you want. Your goal is to get 100% of the students ready for today's lesson; and, on certain days, you may accomplish that goal. But on many more days, you will help some students become ready for today's lesson, while others, even with extra instruction, will be closer, but not completely there. That's okay. It is still a good use of your time to spend a few minutes after the feedback cycle in helping the students who did not do the independent practice correctly to correct their mistakes and get ready for today's lesson. That's a great use of a few minutes of your class time, and it can make all of the difference in the effectiveness of today's lesson. That's the fifth and final opportunity for you to maximize instruction in your class.

SPLITTING YOUR CLASS INTO GROUPS

A word on splitting your class intro groups... I believe that any day you have your entire class doing the exact same activity, you have not maximized learning in your classroom. I have never met a class where all of the students are operating on the exact same level and all the students learned at the exact same rate. I've never seen a class where all the students walk in the door with the exact same level of background information. Because of this, I think it is essential that you become comfortable breaking your class into two groups. I'm not asking you to manage 30 different assignments with 30 students. I'm not even asking you to manage four or six different small groups in your classroom. I'm asking you to become comfortable breaking your class into two groups and having those two groups do two different activities.

On the first day of school, you may not be able to do this. You have not yet taught your class about their individual differences. You haven't taught them the rules or routines of your class. You haven't taught them important things like, *when you're finished with the work that I have given you, what should you do?* If you have a question and I'm helping someone else, what should you do? If your group finishes what they're supposed to do, what is okay to do and what is it not okay to do? You need to pre-teach all of these things to your class before you break them into two groups.

However, once you teach those things to your class, you are able to break your class into two groups. Many of the opportunities to maximize instruction in your classroom involve you breaking your class into two groups and saying, "Some of you are going to do one activity, while others are going to do a different activity." Until you can do this, you cannot really maximize learning in your classroom.

I understand that this causes classroom management issues for some. Due to the age or behavior of your students, you might not feel comfortable breaking your class into two groups. Other factors may cause you to be uncomfortable or hesitant, like the size of your classroom, the organization of your classroom, and the space that you have available.

Even if you don't yet feel comfortable breaking your classroom into two groups, it's important that doing so becomes a goal that you continually work toward.

As long as your entire class is working on only one activity at the same time, you will never be able to maximize the learning in your classroom. The students who are ahead cannot advance. They might quickly grow bored. The students who are behind will struggle and won't be able to grasp the knowledge or skill you're teaching. They will become frustrated and encounter problems when they need that skill or knowledge to apply to future lessons. Both groups cannot maximize their learning experience.

However, the moment you split your class into two groups and have half your class doing one activity and another group in your class doing a different activity, you allow more instruction, more learning, more motivation, and more engagement to occur in your classroom. As a result, you will have maximized the instruction of your class.

Five Opportunities: Putting It All Together

Those are the five opportunities to maximize instruction that happen in every lesson. You'll note that they have some things in common. Many of them ask you to divide your class into two groups. Some of the students will be ready for the next component in your lesson, and others will not. In many cases, you will take five minutes or less to deliver extra instruction to those students who are not ready for the next component.

In some of these cases, the students who are ready for the next component will actually move into the next component while you do that instruction. In other cases, those students will have free time to use wisely while you re-teach other students. Sometimes this will cause classroom management issues that did not exist before, which is why it is important that you pre-teach to your classroom about their individual differences, letting them know what they should do when they complete their assigned work. Make sure they know what they are allowed to do during their free time. What is appropriate, and what is inappropriate?

It is also possible that you might determine that you can only use some of these five methods due to the age and/or behavior of your students or the subject that you teach. That's fine. There is no requirement to use all five of these opportunities, but every time you build one of these opportunities to maximize instruction into your lesson, learning goes up, engagement goes up, motivation goes up, and students learn more.

I don't expect that all five of these will be present in every one of your lessons. Instead, look at each lesson and ask yourself, "Are there one or two opportunities to maximize instruction that I can build into each lesson?" If you do that each day, your class will become more comfortable when some of the students are working on one activity and other students are working on a different activity. Every time you break your class into groups, they become more comfortable, more skilled, and more ready for it to happen again. Done correctly, your students will move onto their next class and say, "Why are we all doing the same thing? That doesn't maximize instruction." They should be prepared to be broken into groups based on their readiness for the next component of the lesson. As a teacher, you should pre-teach and be ready to teach them the skills that are necessary to function in a classroom where that happens. If you add this to your classroom repertoire— to the menu of options available to you as you plan a lesson—motivation and engagement will go up and the actual learning that takes place in your classroom will increase. That's how you maximize full-class instruction.

Chapter Five

FIVE MODELS OF FULL-CLASS INSTRUCTION

This chapter will explain five different models of full-class instruction. Before we begin, there are two things you should know:

First, I don't expect you to use all five of these models. So if you look at one and say, "I couldn't do that because of the subject I teach," or "I couldn't do that because of the grade level I teach," that's okay. That's why there are five of them. You may look at the first one and say, "I can't do that one, but the other four will work for me."

The second thing I will tell you about them is that I don't expect you to use them every single day. There isn't a teaching technique in the world that's good enough to use every single day. Sometimes teachers will look at one of these techniques, and say, "Wow, the kids would get bored with that after 20 days." But kids will get bored with anything after 20 days. That's why you vary what you do in class every day, and you also pick and choose techniques to use occasionally. I don't expect you to use these techniques every day. Instead, I would expect you to look at your week and say, "You know, on Thursday, I could use one of those five models."

Model #1:
AA – Assess and Adjust

The first model is AA, Assess and Adjust. This model includes four steps.

The first step is to teach what you want the students to learn. I assume most teachers would automatically do this sometime during the day, but I know that's not always the case.

After you teach it, you can assign practice, using the same materials you were going to use in the past. You don't have to develop new materials.

We are going to assign less than in the past, meaning a shorter practice assignment, and when the students finish it, we're going to assess to see how they did on it.

Then we're going to assign unique practice to different students in class as our final step.

How does this look in real life? Well, let's take a look at a typical lesson on adverbs. I typically spend 20 minutes at the beginning of class teaching adverbs. And then I have the best worksheet I've ever seen—40 sentences where students circle the adverbs in each sentence.

So how is this class different now that I'm using this AA technique?

Well, I'm still going to teach for 20 minutes on adverbs, what they are, how to use them, how to identify one, and what a good one looks like.

Then I'm going to still use the same worksheet. I'm going to pass the worksheet out to everybody. But instead of assigning 1 through 40, like I have for the last 12 years, I'm going to ask everybody to do 1 through 3. And when they're finished with that, I'll have them show it to me.

Now, some of my students learned adverbs last year. They're done in 30 seconds. When they bring it up, all three are perfect.

Should I assign those students Questions 4 through 40? No. They already know how to do this. Giving them 37 more opportunities to practice a skill they already know is a recipe for a student who hates school, and who never reaches their full potential, because I was too inflexible to change my assignment for certain students.

Instead, that student needs an assignment which extends the learning or applies the learning to a new situation.

After five minutes, a student brings up their worksheet, and they've done two of the three correctly.

I've got two concerns here. They're doing the worksheet pretty slowly, almost too slowly to be useful. And they aren't getting them all right. So that student does need more practice. I might assign that student Questions 4 through 20 and then check back with them.

And after 15 minutes, there's a student who hasn't gotten out of their desk yet. I go to their desk. They've done number 1 and gotten it wrong. They're halfway done with number 2, and they're getting it wrong. They haven't even started number 3 yet. Should I assign that student Questions 4 through 40? No. They don't know how to do this.

Asking them to do it wrong 37 more times is a recipe for a frustrated student who hates school and eventually drops out of school. Instead, that student needs either practice on prerequisite skills or more instruction on today's learning objective. And luckily, I'm now in a system where everyone else is working on something, so I have a little bit of time to give him more targeted instruction.

And in one class, with one teacher and 30, 35, I've done this with 40 students, you have a lesson that meets the learning needs of your most gifted student and your most struggling student, without the need for assistance from additional people. There's no aid in this classroom; there's no special education teacher in this classroom. There is only one teacher meeting the individual needs of 35 students.

Common Questions

Question: Isn't this more work?

Answer: That's a great question. One of the objections is that it's more work. So let's take a look at that.

First of all, we're going to teach, and we're going to teach it the way we've always taught it. So that's nothing new, you were going to do that, anyway.

Second, you want to assign practice. You can use the same practice you've been using for the last 10 years. So that's not more work.

What we do need is an extension assignment, an assignment for students who are well above grade level or who already know the subject, and we need a remedial assignment. Now the remedial assignment really isn't new. It's probably just practice from what we were doing a week ago or two weeks ago. But some people would consider that the development of new material.

Most publishers today include an extension assignment and a remedial assignment in every single lesson when they publish a curriculum. If you're hesitant to use those, then you will have to develop them on your own.

That's why I wouldn't recommend you use this technique every single day for the rest of the school year. Instead, I recommend that you look at your lesson plans for the next three weeks and try to find one time during those three weeks when you can do this. . Then you have three weeks to plan what your extension assignment will be and what you remedial assignment will be. By working ahead in three-week segments, you will have time to prepare those two extra assignments.

The neat thing is, next year when you come back to this lesson, those will already be done and ready to go for you. And if you do this just once a month for the rest of the school year, and next year you do it once a month during the school year, and the following year you did it just once a month, pretty soon, three times out of every month, three of your lessons would actually meet the individual needs of the students in front of you.

I agree, if you had to do this every single day with every lesson that you taught, this would become an overwhelming burden. But if you utilize the existing resources that your publisher provides, create some of your own resources, and try to do it once a month, it really becomes something that you can do.

Then, next year when you come back to those lessons, those lessons are already to go. More and more, you'll be meeting the individual needs of the students you have in front of you.

Question: Won't students intentionally get some items wrong on the initial assignment so that they get an easier assignment in the end?

Answer: Okay, the question is about a student who recognizes that if they get them wrong, they get easier work. So they tank the initial assessment. That is a great question. It is another reason why teachers don't use this technique every day.

If teachers use this every day, they may find a pattern of students who tank the initial assessment and do poorly on it intentionally, so that they can do a different assignment. It's important when you design the different assignments for this model, that you don't make the extension or challenging assignment seem harder, longer, or like a lot more work.

Oftentimes, this extension assignment seems more fun and more creative. And given the choice between doing drill and practice assignments, practicing a specific skill, or actually applying a skill that the student already knows, students again and again choose to do the assignment where they get to apply the skill in a creative way, rather than just practice the skill again and again.

So teachers won't use this every day because kids will catch on. They'll use it sporadically so that kids won't catch on. If you have particular students who do catch on and often tank the initial assessment, teachers will deal with that by cloaking the initial assessment in another assignment or another assessment.

For instance, the Chapter 3 test might have three questions on it that are really pre-questions for whatever we're doing the next day. Or today's assignment might have two questions on it that are really preparing for what we're going to do tomorrow and choosing your assignment for the next day, but they're kind of cloaked in a previous assessment or a previous assignment.

Question: What do you do with students who finish the work, but then begin to misbehave when you're helping someone else?

Answer: In a perfect world, everybody works quietly with their heads down at their desks so you can provide 30 minutes of additional instruction to other students. In a perfect world. But I don't live in that world. In my world, kids are coming up to me all the time.

The one technique teachers use again and again, that pays off every single day of the whole school year, is *pre-teaching* to students what they should do in certain situations.

For instance, in your class by this time in the school year, you should have already pre-taught to your students, "When you finish your work, and it appears that you don't have anything else to do in my class, what should you do?"

You have options. If you walked up to every student and asked, "What are your options when you finish work early?," they should know what they can and cannot do. They should know because you've taught them—you've practiced with them. You've quizzed them on it. You know who knows it, and you know who doesn't.

When that happens in some classes, I can pull out a book and read it. In some classes when that happens, I can work on another subject area. In some classes, I can go to the back of the room where there are learning stations with fun things that I can do. In some classes, there are a couple of computers that I can use and am allowed to log into my Facebook page and update it.

Whatever it is that your students can do when they finish their work in your class should be pre-taught to students.

The other thing that teachers pre-teach answers this question: "When I'm working with a student and you have a question, what should you do?"

You should not walk up and interrupt me when I'm helping another student. That is not what you should do. The first thing you should do is this... The second thing you should do is ask the person sitting next to you, the third thing you should do is...

I talked to a teacher who told me she has three kids in her class wear visors every day, and those are the three that know today's objectives. So if other students have a question, they can always ask one of the students wearing a visor. That's why they have the visors on.

What if students do all of those things and still can't figure out the answer? What should they do?

Should they raise your hand and wait for me to see it? Should they come up and tell me they need my help when I get a chance? Or should they pull out a book and just start reading something else until I'm free?

Teachers who pre-teach things like this—telling students what to do when they're finished, what to do when they have a question and the teacher is working with somebody else—have a whole new array of strategies they can use with their students.

Teachers who don't pre-teach these things try these strategies once, say that it created chaos, and never try them again. But it's not that it didn't work because the technique is bad—it didn't work because the teacher didn't do the pre-teaching, letting students know what to do in different situations.

Question: How do I grade with this technique?

Answer: There's a mistake that teachers make in grading, and that is to grade *during* the learning process.

Oftentimes, we teach students a new skill, and then we immediately give them an assignment to practice that skill. What is the purpose of that practice assignment? The purpose of the practice assignment is so the student can acquire the new skill.

You should not grade that practice assignment for accuracy, because if you do, you're grading them while they are learning the new skill. And your grade book is a terribly inaccurate reflection of what the student knows and doesn't know.

It's like putting a rain gauge out in the middle of a rainstorm and then pulling it in while it's still raining and saying, "Oh! Only a half inch of rain. I guess the weathermen were wrong!" But it's still pouring down rain!

You're doing the same thing when you teach a student a new skill, immediately give them a practice assignment, and then grade that practice assignment on accuracy.

Teachers who do that are not using a research supported practice. And they will struggle in a differentiated classroom.

On the other hand, most teachers have addressed this situation by grading that first practice assignment for completion. "I want you to try all of these items so you get good at these new skills. Understanding that, you're going to get some of them wrong and some of them right, and I'm going to give you feedback. I'm going to correct it and give you feedback. But the grade that I enter into the grade book is going to be on whether or not you tried them all."

If you grade with this research supported practice, you won't struggle in a differentiated classroom, because you'll be grading each student's different assignment on whether or not they completed it.

Model #2:
BB – Begin and Branch

The second lesson design model is BB, Begin and Branch.

In this method, you start by teaching your students today's objective. By the way, we're going to teach it fast, as fast as your fastest student in class might learn it.

Then, there's going to be a pivotal moment when I ask my class to show me whether or not they understand, or know, or can do today's objective. Those who can do it will begin independent practice immediately. Those who cannot do it will receive more instruction and have another opportunity to show me whether or not they can do it.

This breaks the class into two groups: those who have today's objective and can begin practice, and those who don't and need more instruction.

So how does this really look?

Well, I start by teaching, just like I always did, 20 minutes of instruction, but I do it fast. I compress it into five minutes—super-fast, as fast as I think my fastest learner can get it.

Then, there's this pivotal moment. I'd like everybody to show me what they know. And in this one example, I'm actually going to move the kids around the classroom.

If you can show me that you know today's objective, you're going to move to the back of the classroom and begin independent practice. If you don't know today's objective, you're going to move to the front of the classroom, and I'm going to teach you for 10 more minutes.

After 10 more minutes of instruction, I'm going to check again. Do you know today's objective? If you do, you can join the people in the back of the classroom. If you don't, then I'm going to teach you for five more minutes.

By now, the group's down to five. So that group can just come around my table up here and after five more minutes, three of you are going to join the back group. It's just me and two students now, and I'm able to give individualized help to the students who need it.

Some students in my class get a lot of instruction. Some students get less instruction with one teacher in one classroom.

Everywhere I go, I ask teachers a question. "Do you believe that students learn at different rates?" And everywhere I go, teachers nod their heads like bobble head dolls.

I was at a school the other day, and I said, "Raise your hand if you believe that students learn at different rates." Every hand in the room went up. Every teacher believes that students learn at different rates.

So I picked out one of the teachers and asked, "Yesterday in your class, how many minutes of instruction did your fastest learner get?" He was a math teacher, and he thought about it for a second and said, "Yesterday, in my class, my fastest learner got 17 minutes of instruction." I said, "Okay, yesterday in class, how many minutes of instruction did your slowest learner get?" And do you know what he said? "17 minutes of instruction."

So you really don't believe that students learn at different rates, do you? Because if you did, you wouldn't give the fastest learner in your class and the slowest learner in your class the exact same minutes of instruction every day.

In this method, with one teacher in one classroom with 35 students, no aids, no extra help, no special education teacher, I'm able to give my fastest learner five minutes of instruction and my slowest learner 35 minutes of instruction in a way that is manageable and doable for a single teacher without a need for extra help.

Question: What if a student pretends that they understand just to get the practice assignment?

Answer: This question is about a student who fakes their way into independent practice. That's why the students don't get to choose the group. The students have to show you what they know in some sort of assessment and you have to verify that they know it. Then they can join that other group.

Question: What if I am teaching content, rather than a skill?

Answer: This is a better technique to use on those days that you're teaching skills. Even within a course like history that is heavy on facts and content, there are skills that are essential—cause and effect, identifying main ideas, summarizing things, and supporting details with an argument. I would use this technique on days when you're teaching skill-based things, over days when you're just having them memorize facts. When I look at my lesson plans over the next couple of weeks, I'll always have days where I'm just doing what you're talking about, and days where I'm teaching skills. This technique works better on your skill-based days.

Question: Isn't there a stigma attached to being in the last group?

Answer: Teachers are sometimes worried about students who end up in that last group. They're concerned that they're the last ones to learn it, and the rest of the class can see that they are the last ones to learn it. And they're worried about that.

I want to share with you my experience with this, because I don't want you to be reluctant to use this technique because you're worried students will be ostracized or feel badly if they're in that last group.

My experience is that the slowest learners in your classroom already know that they're the slowest learners in your classroom. My experience is that the fastest learners in your classroom already know who the fastest learners in your classroom are. And, the fastest learners in your classroom already know who the slowest learners in your classroom are.

In second grade, my daughter came home and identified all four of the special education students in her class. She knew who they were. Two of them wouldn't be identified by the district for six more years. But she nailed it. She knew it in second grade.

So the groups already know who they are. My question for you is: At your school, do they hate each other yet? Because they will.

I was in the office the other day, waiting to meet with a principal. I was sitting outside his office because he was still on the phone. A student came and sat in the chair next to me. I asked, "What are you doing here?" She looked at me and said, "I'm waiting to see the principal." I said, "Well, so am I." I asked, "Why are you waiting to see the principal?" She looked at me and said, "I hate school." She had anger in her eyes. So I asked, "Why would you hate school?" Her response was telling. "The teacher just keeps talking and talking and talking. I understood it after two minutes, but she had to do five more examples because there's two students in our class who never learn it after the first couple of examples."

A dynamic that's present in a lot of classrooms around the country is that students do not want to have homework. What determines whether or not you have homework? What determines whether or not you have homework is when the teacher begins independent practice.

If the teacher passes out independent practice with 10 minutes left in class, we're not going to have homework because I can finish it up in the last 10 minutes of class. On the other hand, the worst thing in the world is when the teacher stands by the door with the worksheet and as her students walk out, she hands them the worksheet. You know you're going to have homework that night because she passed it out.

Actually, that's not really the worst thing in the world. The worst thing in the world is when the teacher picks up the worksheets with ten minutes left in class, and she's going to pass them out, and then somebody asks a question! Then, she sets down the worksheets, does three more examples, and then she passes it out as we walk out of the classroom! I hate that student! I hate that student because I wasn't going to have homework until that student asked a question.

Most kids aren't afraid to ask questions in class because they're afraid they'll look stupid. That's not why they don't ask questions in class. They already know they're stupid. Just ask them—they'll tell you—because their parents have been telling them for years, teachers have been sending signals for years, and their friends have been telling them for years. They don't ask questions because they know the moment they raise their hands, what are they going to hear from the rest of the students in class? Moans and groans, of course! That's why they don't ask questions.

With this new BB teaching model, you allow your slower students to get out of the way of the faster students. They're not slowing each other down anymore. And they can actually get the help they need without everybody else in the class hating them because they're slowing down the whole class.

Given the choice between having an assignment that they know how to do and having an assignment that they don't know how to do, 100% of students will choose the assignment they know how to do.

Therefore, putting kids into independent practice before they know how to do something is not something that they want. They want extra instruction so that they will know how to do the assignment. They just don't want to feel like they're slowing down the rest of the class.

This method allows you to do that. Your fastest learner already knows who they are. The slowest learners already know who they are. That's not the question. The question is whether they hate each other yet. If you don't use a technique like this, they will. If you use a technique like this, you'll have less bullying, less harassment, fewer kids making fun of other kids, and less animosity between your fastest learners and your slowest learners.

Model #3:
CC – Creative Choice

The third technique we're going to go over is CC, Creative Choice.

In this technique, you teach today's objective. You do some guided practice. Then, for independent practice, you offer choices: multiple products to choose from for independent practice.

Let me give you an example. For years, you've been teaching the causes of the Civil War, and you've always done it with the Civil War packet. And it's a great packet, by the way. It's one of the best packets ever. In fact, it's in the Packet Hall of Fame.

This year, I just want you to offer choices. Tell the students they can do the packet if they want. And some students will choose that. They're packet masters. That's why they get straight A's.

But I want you to offer a choice, such as "If you don't want to do the packet, you also could give a four-minute presentation to the class on the causes of the Civil War."

You also could let them design a PowerPoint presentation or a Website.

You could do any activity. You could interview the principal — he's a veteran of the Civil War.

You could do any of these activities, and they all would show you that your students understand the causes of the Civil War. And the neat thing is, you don't have to know a single thing about your students.

You don't need to test them for multiple intelligence or learning style. Just lay out the choices. The law of self-preservation says students will choose to show you what they know in the way that they can show you the best.

Now if you've never done anything like this in the past, this is a terrible example because there are four choices, and when you do it, it's going to seem like chaos.

If you've never done anything like this in the past, just one time in the next couple of weeks, pick a day when you were going to give out the same worksheet you always give out, and offer one other choice. "You can do the old worksheet, or you can give a two minute presentation to the class." Just two choices. If you do it with just two choices, you're going to become more and more comfortable with this, and maybe one day you'll expand to three choices and four choices. Maybe not — maybe you'll just stick to two choices. But every time you do, you meet the needs of more students in your classroom.

Model #4
Keyed Activity Assessment

This simple to use and easy to try model of instruction is the Keyed Activity Assessment.

In this method of instruction, you begin by asking your students a question or series of questions. This is called the *Initial Assessment*. On the basis of how they do on this initial assessment, you determine what activity they do next.

The simplest form of this method is to ask your students a question when they walk into your room. If they answer the question correctly, they go into group A. If they answer the question incorrectly, they go into group B. Group A works on the next activity, while group B gets re-taught the original material.

Here is a simple example of Keyed Activity Assessment. When the students come into the room, the teacher asks them to complete this problem:

$$3 + 2 \times 6 =$$

If the students get the correct answer (15), it indicates they understand the concept of "order of operations," and they are assigned Section B. If the students get the incorrect answer, it indicates they do not understand the concept, they are re-taught and are assigned Section A.

Section A:

1) $4 + 5 \times 3 =$

2) $2 + 4 \times 5 =$

3) $12 - 2 \times 4 =$

4) $8 + 5 - 2 =$

5) $4 + 5 \times 6 =$

Section B:

1) $4 + 5 \times 3 + 4 + 5 \times 6 =$

2) $2 + 4 \times 5 + 4 + 5 \times (3 + 4) + 5 \times 6 =$

3) $12 - 2 \times 4 + (2 + 4 \times 5) =$

4) $8 + 5 - 2 + 4 + 5 \times (3 + 2) + 4 \times 5 =$

5) $4 + 5 \times 6 + 2 + 4 \times 5 + (4 + 5) \times 3 + 4 + 5 \times 6 =$

This lesson works because each student is working at his or her own level and maximizing his or her own potential. No one is bored re-learning material they already know, so behavior problems are avoided. No one is lost, working on an assignment they do not understand, so attention and attendance remain high.

On the following page is a chart used to organize Keyed Activity Assessment lessons. You can record the concepts you are trying to teach, the questions you are using to assess learning, and the activities students will do.

Keyed Activity Assessment		
Concept	Question	Activity

The following pages contain numerous examples of lessons using this method. Each of the lessons presented are from real teachers teaching in real classrooms. These lessons work to motivate students and maximize the learning potential of each child.

Keyed Activity Assessment		
Here is an example from an elementary math classroom. You can use it to break your students into two, three, four, or even five different groups.		
Concept	Question	Activity
Multiplication 1's & 2's	1 x 2 =	Flash Cards
Multiplication 3's & 4's	3 x 4 =	Worksheet
Multiplication 5's & 6's	6 x 6 =	Computer Game
Multiplication 7's & 8's	8 x 7 =	Fill in Grid
Multiplication 9's & 10's	9 x 9 =	Homemade Calculator

Five Models of Full-Class Instruction

Keyed Activity Assessment

This example comes right out of a science classroom, teaching students with a wide variety of science backgrounds about density.

Concept	Question	Activity
Solve for D	M = 6g V = 200 ml D = ?	Worksheet 1
Solve for M	M = ? V = 200 ml D = 2.5 g/ml	Worksheet 2
Solve for V	M = 6g V = ? D = 3.5 g/ml	Worksheet 3
Find the Density Lab		Lab 1

Keyed Activity Assessment

People ask me all the time about how to effectively use aides or parent volunteers in the classroom. This teacher used the extra adult to help after doing an initial assessment.

Concept	Question	Activity
Short u words	Fill in your own assessments	Work with Mrs. Johnson
Short o words		Worksheet
Short a words		Card Game
Short e words		Matching Packet
Short i words		Book

Keyed Activity Assessment

This Algebra teacher spent years teaching these four concepts over the course of a week. The rigid pacing created boredom and behavior problems. Now, she does an initial assessment and allows students to focus on the concepts they do not know. She teaches the same material in about half the time.

Concept	Question	Activity
One-Step Addition	$X + 2 = 7$	Worksheet #1
One-Step Subtraction	$X - 3 = 9$	Worksheet #2
One-Step Multiplication	$4x = 24$	Worksheet #3
One-Step Division	$X/4 = 8$	Worksheet #4

Keyed Activity Assessment

U.S. History can utilize this technique in many ways. Here is an example of splitting a class into two, three, four, or even five groups based on the concepts the students are struggling with. Start small and split into two groups. Get comfortable and try even more!

Concept	Question	Activity
Causes	Fill in your own assessments	Video
Countries		Map Activity
Leaders		Packet
Battles		Computer Simulation
Homefront		Play

Model #5:
Workdown Bin

While the Keyed Activity Assessment is a great tool to differentiate based on the difference in background information, it does not do much to adjust for rate of learning. For this, you need a second method.

A Workdown Bin is a series of activities your students do in order. There is no time frame given for moving from one activity to another. When the students have completed one activity, they move on to the next.

This allows each student to spend the correct amount of time on each activity. If we really believe that students learn at different rates, then we need to stop putting them on our schedule and let them work on their own schedule. Workdown Bin allows you to do this in an organized and manageable way.

The simplest Workdown Bin is to give students one activity, and when they are done, they know to move on to a second activity. The teacher's instructions might include, "Finish reading the story, and when you complete that, you should begin the worksheet."

This type of instruction differentiates on the basis of rate of learning because the students are able to comfortably complete one assignment before moving on to the next.

The chart on the next page is used to organize a Workdown Bin lesson. You can record the concepts you are trying to teach, as well as the activities students will do.

Workdown Bin	
Concept	**Activity**

The following pages contain numerous examples of lessons using this method. Each of the lessons presented here are from real teachers teaching in real classrooms. These lessons work to motivate students and maximize the learning potential of each child.

Here is an economics lesson that allows some students to advance quickly through the introductory material, while other students spend more time grasping these concepts. Using this lesson, the number of classroom discipline problems decreased and student comprehension and achievement increased. The teacher kept the class on this set of activities for three class periods.

Workdown Bin	
Economics	
Concept	**Activity**
Stock Prices	Stock Market Board Game
Dividends	Simulation Activity
Valuation	Newspaper Activity
P/E Ratio	Worksheet
Picking Good Stocks	Internet Stock Market Game

The following lesson once again allows the students to advance at their own rate of learning. The teacher can remain on this set of activities for a flexible period of time, but it is important to note that all students are not expected to progress to the last activity. Students learn at different rates, and that is okay. You will quickly get a feel for when it is time to move on to a new set of activities.

Workdown Bin	
Language Arts	
Concept	**Activity**
Recognizing Letters	Flashcards
Writing Letters	Worksheet
Recognizing Sounds	Tape recorder activity
Speaking Sounds	Work with Mrs. Johnson
Identifying objects beginning with sounds	Scavenger Hunt

This Geometry lesson was traditionally taught over five days, even though many of the students had already been exposed to much of the information. Using the Workdown Bin below, the teacher spent just three days on the material and student achievement increased.

Workdown Bin	
Multi-Concept	
Geometry	
Concept	**Activity**
Area of a Rectangle	Fill in your own activities
Area of a Triangle	
Area of a Circle	
Area of a Pentagon	
Area of a *Regular Polygon*	

Here is a Workdown Bin you can use for almost any set of concepts, or even when teaching just one concept to your students. Remember, you would not use a Keyed Activity Assessment or Workdown Bin every day with your students. Use them occasionally as appropriate and you will find them a valuable addition to your teaching arsenal.

Workdown Bin	
Continuum	**Activity**
	Crossword Puzzle
	Fill-in-the-blank worksheet
	Short Answer Activity
	Essay Questions
	Extended Role-Play

Final Thoughts on Five Models of Full-Class Instruction

Improving instruction is difficult. One of the dynamics that makes improvement so difficult is that your current methods are not failing. They are working with up to 80%, or even 90%, of your students. This makes change difficult because you risk lowering that number.

But remember this: by not changing, you never have a chance to raise that number. Also remember this: if you do try a new technique and it does not work, you can always go back to your old method of teaching.

By showing you five research-based techniques to improve your instruction in the classroom, I hope this chapter has planted a seed. You many never fully adopt one of these models, but you very well may use strategies and concepts from within them.

However you choose to use this material, be willing to try new techniques and strategies to better meet the needs of students in your classroom.

Chapter Six

PUTTING IT ALL TOGETHER

Two words describe great teaching to me: Continual Improvement.

No teacher is perfect...but the great ones are constantly trying to improve. This chapter will conclude with some simple activities you can do to continually expand your arsenal of teaching techniques.

It is my hope that you will use all of the chapters in the book to expand your teaching methods and try new techniques. Each day, your goal should be to meet the needs of every student in your classroom. And every day, your goal should be to become a better teacher than you were yesterday.

I wish you well on this journey.

Pat

Expand Your Arsenal

Let's begin by expanding your arsenal. Every teacher has a certain number of tricks up their sleeve—the teaching techniques they use to help students learn. When was the last time you learned some new tricks?

This exercise is meant to help you grow. Begin by looking at the list of different ways to deliver content. First, go through the list and circle each method if you use this method with your students. When you have completed that assessment, go through the list again and place a check mark next to any methods that are not circled which you would be willing to try. Try to select three new methods of content delivery that you could use in the next month.

You can also add methods you use that are not on the list to the bottom of the list. Repeat this exercise monthly to continually expand your arsenal of content delivery techniques.

Methods of Content Delivery	
bulletin boards	radio
banners	tapes
posters	blog
television	television
slides	lectures
website	debates
flashcards	discussions
transparencies	field trips
drama	drama
comics	readings
objects	interviews
community events	letters

Other:

This next exercise is meant to help you expand the number of ways you have students practice.

First, go through the list and circle each method if you use this method with your students. When you have completed that assessment, go through the list again and place a check mark next to any methods that are not circled which you would be willing to try. Try to select three new methods of student practice that you could use in the next month.

You can also add methods you use that are not on the list to the bottom of the list. Repeat this exercise monthly to continually expand your arsenal.

Verbalize	Write	Create	Perform	Solve
oral report	theme	diorama	simulation	puzzles
panel discussion	research	collage	role play	mazes
debate	paper	website	drama	problems
open discussion	report	painting	concert	equations
games	workbook	model	model	riddles
brainstorm	chalkboard	graph	music	games
oral questions &	poems	pictograph	dance	brainteasers
answers	essays	mural	pantomime	scavenger
telephone	stories	maps	puppet	hunt
interviews	diary	power point	shows	charades
commentary	books	food	radio	
	plays	timelines	commercials	
	cookbook	clothing		
	blog	bulletin board		
	email	banner		
		movie/video		
		presentation		
		portraits		
		games		
		inventions		

This next exercise is meant to help you expand the number of ways you evaluate student learning.

First, go through the list and circle each method if you use this method with your students. When you have completed that assessment, go through the list again and place a check mark next to any methods that are not circled which you would be willing to try. Try to select three new methods of evaluating student learning that you could use in the next month.

You can also add methods you use that are not on the list to the bottom of the list. Repeat this exercise monthly to continually expand your arsenal.

Methods of Evaluating Student Learning	
self evaluation	draw pictures
Know-Want to Know-Learned	take home test
Online quiz	extended or no time line
email	open book
peer evaluation	journal
work samples	rubric
video	poster
spot checks	website
portfolio	checklist
tests	presentation
dictate	project
oral	authentic
interview	create a test
Other:	

Appendix A

DIFFERENTIATION
SELF-ASSESSMENT

The following "Differentiation Inventory" is provided to help you examine your current practices.

The tool will look at four different types of student differences:

> Background Information
>
> Rate of Learning
>
> Learning Style
>
> Personal Interest

You should keep all four of these differences in mind as you design each Tier One Lesson.

Differentiation Inventory

Here is a listing of four different ways to meet the individual needs of your students. Below each one is a chance for you to give yourself a rating from one to ten. There is also space below this rating for you to write down the actions you currently take or need to take to meet the needs of students in this area.

Background Information

Every time you walk into the classroom to teach something to your students, some of them already know everything you are going to say. Every time you walk into the classroom to teach something to your students, some of them don't know anything about what you are going to say. Students have different levels of background information, and every time we try to teach anything to them, we need to not only keep this in mind, but also do something about it. I recommend doing two things: Communicate that you recognize their range of differences, and then tell them what your plan is to deal with it.

Rate yourself of accommodating differences in Background
Information   1   2   3   4   5   6   7   8   9   10

Notes: _____

_____

_____

Rate of Learning

Some students learn new material the first time they are exposed to it, while others take multiple exposures to the same information before they learn it. Students learn at different rates and every time we try to teach anything to them we need to not only keep this in mind, but also do something about it. I recommend doing two things: Communicate that you recognize their range of differences, and then tell them what your plan is to deal with it.

Rate yourself of accommodating differences in Rate of Learning

1   2   3   4   5   6   7   8   9   10

Notes: _____

_____

_____

Learning Style

Students learn in different ways. Some students learn by listening, some by watching, still others by actively participating. Students have different learning styles, and every time we try to teach anything to them, we need to not only keep this in mind, but also do something about it. I recommend doing two things: Communicate that you recognize their range of differences, and then tell them what your plan is to deal with it.

Rate yourself of accommodating differences in Learning Style

1   2   3   4   5   6   7   8   9   10

Notes: _____

_____

_____

Personal Interest

Students have differences in personal interests. Some of your students are interested in cars, while others like dolls. Some of your students are interested in sports, while others like music. Students have different interests, and every time we try to teach anything to them, we need to not only keep this in mind, but also do something about it. I recommend doing two things: Communicate that you recognize their range of differences, and then tell them what your plan is to deal with it.

Rate yourself of accommodating differences in Personal Interest

1   2   3   4   5   6   7   8   9   10

Notes: _____

_____

_____

Does this describe your teaching?

❑ Teachers begin where the students are

❑ Teachers engage students in instruction through different learning modalities

❑ A student competes more against himself or herself than others

❑ Teachers provide specific ways for each individual to learn

❑ Teachers use classroom time flexibly

❑ Teachers are diagnosticians, prescribing the best possible instruction for each student

❑ Instruction is concept focused and principle driven

❑ Ongoing assessment of student readiness and growth are built into the curriculum

❑ Flexible grouping is consistently used

❑ Students are active explorers

Appendix B

OVERVIEW OF RTI

This book has focused on a very specific part of Response to Intervention: Tier One Full-Class Instruction.

Tier One is just one piece of a much larger puzzle. To help you understand where Tier One Full-Class Instruction fits within the larger context of RTI, I provide this overview of Response to Intervention.

Response to Intervention: A Simple Explanation Introduction

One of the biggest reasons that schools do not successfully implement Response to Intervention is due to how they are exposed to Response to Intervention for the very first time.

How you teach your teachers about RTI, how you expose them to it, how you tell them about it, and how you frame the whole concept of Response to Intervention will make all of the difference in the world when it comes to whether or not your school will be successful in implementing RTI.

I have often told people that when I first heard about RTI, I read three books on the topic and I was more confused than ever. I attended two big conferences on RTI, and I still had no idea what I was supposed to do differently in my classroom! This is the experience I hear from teachers around the country—that the more professional development they get on RTI, the more confused, the more scared, and the more underequipped they feel to implement Response to Intervention.

I believe one of the best ways that you can help your school be successful in its RTI implementation is to have a simple explanation for RTI for your teachers. I use a simple step-by-step explanation that walks teachers through the RTI process. I don't use any pyramids or triangles, and I rarely use the word "tier" because none of these things will help teachers understand what they need to do to implement RTI.

I am now going to share with you my simple explanation of Response to Intervention.

I do this for two reasons: because I'd like to show you how simple you can make Response to Intervention for your teachers, and also to model for you a way of explaining it, framing it, and teaching it to your teachers. This method of explanation will allow them to easily understand RTI, not be afraid of it, and actually believe that they are empowered to implement it.

Step 1: *Universal Screening*

Response to Intervention begins with a Universal Screening, and by definition, the Universal Screening is given to all students. The purpose of the Universal Screening—the only purpose of a Universal Screening— is to identify which students you are going to monitor more closely during Tier One interventions. That's the only purpose of it.

The purpose of the Universal Screening is not to put students into groups. The purpose of the Universal Screening is not to say if you do really well on the Universal Screening, you are not in an intervention group—if you do poorly, you're in a Tier One Intervention—if you do really poorly, you're in a Tier Two Intervention—if you do terrible on it, you are in a Tier Three Intervention. That's not a Universal Screening; that is a Placement Test. If you are using your Universal Screening to place students in groups, it is a Placement Test, not an RTI Universal Screening.

So the Universal Screening is given to all students. Some schools do it once a year; some schools do it twice a year; some schools do it as often as four times per year for all students so they have scores indicating where all students are performing, what skills they have and what skills they don't in a particular area. Remember, the only purpose of this is to identify which students you are going to monitor more closely during the Tier One Intervention. Most schools that I know are already doing a Universal Screening; this is not something new.

Please note that this is one of the most important concepts when you're teaching teachers about Response to Intervention. Remind them that they are already doing many parts of RTI, and that's a clear message I want to send about the Universal Screening—you are already doing this. It is something your school already does. You already have test scores for your students, so this is nothing new. This is not an add on; this is not more work for you; this is not more paperwork for you. You already give all of your students a test to measure their skill levels, I assume at the beginning of the year or at the end of the previous school year, and that is a Universal Screening.

Step 2: *Tier One Full-Class Intervention*

The second step of Response to Intervention is the Tier One full-class intervention. The full-class interventions are done with a full class of students, and most teachers that I know are already teaching to a full class, at least occasionally. I hope they are, anyway!

When you explain RTI to teachers, you want to be sure to point out to them that you are already doing this — you are already teaching to your full class. That's what a Tier One Intervention is: full-class instruction. And so, when you stand up and teach a curriculum, a lesson, a skill, or some knowledge to your full class, that's a Tier One Full-class Intervention.

The only thing to add here to make this fit within the RTI context is that you want to make sure you're using a *research-validated curriculum.*

Now, research-validated, or research-proven, is a new barrier to go over. It used to be that you could choose any curriculum that you knew that worked or that a neighboring district told you had worked, and that is simply not good enough anymore.

It used to be that you could have a research-based curriculum, a curriculum that was based on someone else's research. That's not good enough anymore. The legislation that brought RTI into existence says that you should be using a research-validated (or research-proven) intervention, instruction, or curriculum, which means that an independent third party should have data to show that this intervention actually works.

Now, most of you are already using a research-validated curriculum in the areas of Reading and Mathematics, and so the one message that I want to make sure I send to teachers on this step is that you are already doing this. You'd want to double-check the curriculum that you're using...but if you're using a major textbook publisher, I can tell you as soon as this legislation came out, they all scrambled to get studies done to show that their curriculum worked, and most of them have passed that barrier.

Step 3: *Fidelity Check*

The next step is the Fidelity Check during the full-class intervention. The Fidelity Check is having another adult come into the room and observe the teaching and make sure that it is being taught correctly.

Fidelity is just a fancy word that says, "Is the curriculum being delivered in the way that it was research-proven to work?" So, you want to have another adult come in and watch the teacher teach the curriculum.

I'd be willing to bet many of you are already doing this. Every school that I've ever taught in has administrators going around and observing teachers, especially new teachers. These observations are documented, which is another thing that you want to do during your Fidelity Check.

Most teachers are already observed teaching, and that observation is documented for some reason at the school and kept in the administrator's office at the school, so you are already doing this.

So we are now three steps into Response to Intervention, and we haven't done anything new yet!

Step Four: *Progress Monitoring*

That brings us to the next step: progress monitoring during Tier One, and this is new.

Let me say it again—this is the first step that is new for most of your teachers, and this is the spot where most schools fall apart during Response to Intervention.

Progress Monitoring: What is it? It is to measure the progress of certain students during the instruction.

So you're going to instruct over a period of time (four weeks, maybe six weeks), and you are going to measure the progress of certain students.

Do you measure the progress of all students? No.

Which students do you measure? You measure the progress of the students identified in the Universal Screening (remember, that was the purpose of the Universal Screening).

You want to monitor progress over time, which means, periodically, you want to measure the progress of those students.

Let's say you give a Universal Screening. You identify four students in your class who need to be monitored more closely. You begin full-class instruction, and, two times a week, you monitor the progress of those students with a progress-monitoring tool.

It is the school's responsibility to provide a progress-monitoring tool for the teachers and teach them how to use it.

The data from this progress monitoring, which should be done a minimum of two times a week over four to six weeks, should be recorded and graphed, and this is new for teachers.

In the past, teachers used to be able to call the assistant principal or call the Special Education Department and say, "I have a student in class, and he needs extra help. He needs to be referred for Special Education." And the person on the other end of the phone would ask, "How do you know?" The teacher would reply, "I can tell. I've been doing this for 20 years. I can tell." That used to be good enough, but not anymore.

Response to Intervention requires that you have data to show whether or not the student is learning during the intervention that you are delivering, and so this is a new requirement.

Colleges aren't teaching it. Graduate courses are rarely teaching it. Teachers aren't trained in this; they don't know where to find the tools, how to use the tools, how to record the data from the tools, and how to graph the tools. So you want to focus your professional development efforts on this step.

This is where schools will fall apart. You want to make sure you make this as simple as possible for teachers.

What makes progress monitoring work is that you're measuring the same thing every time. Some teachers come to me and ask, "Aren't we already doing progress monitoring? I give the chapter 1 test; I give the chapter 2 test; I give the chapter 3 test; I give the chapter 4 test."

Or another teacher will come to me and say, "I give a spelling test every Friday. Isn't that progress monitoring?"

The answer to both of those questions is no.

It's not progress monitoring because you're measuring a different thing every time.

What makes progress monitoring progress monitoring is that you're measuring the same thing every time.

Does that mean you're using the same items? No.

If you're testing sight words, for instance, you're not using the same set of 10 sight words, but the sight words all are at the same level.

If you're having a student read a passage, it doesn't have to be the same reading passage every time, but the passage should always be at the same level, often out of the same book.

If you're measuring math facts, you don't get the same math facts every time, but the math facts should be from the same level. If you're checking multiplication facts from 0 through 9, you should check that every time.

This should be done periodically, at least two times a week. Some people do it more often.

You're gathering data points on your graph. You don't want to make a decision until you have 10 to 12 data points, so how often should you do it?

Well, if you do it once a week, this is going to take you 12 weeks. If you did it just twice a week, it would only take you 6 weeks.

And that's why we recommend 2 to 3 times a week, because it gets you to the decision-making point even faster.

Of course, you could take it to its extreme and say, "Well, if all I need is 12 data points, why don't I do it at 9:00, 10:00, 11:00, 1:00, and 2:00? In three days, I'd have enough data!" While that might be a nice idea and you would have lots of data points, you have to remember, this is done during the intervention, so you have to give some time for teaching to take place for this to happen.

The progress monitoring is done 2 to 3 times a week until you have 12 to 15 data points that you can graph. You're going to graph them over time, and you are going to put a dot on the graph for each time you've monitored progress and connect the dots.

This will give you a line. The line will either be going up over time, be going straight—level—over time, or be going down over time. It is now decision-making time.

If the line is going up, the intervention is working, and you should keep doing it until the student has reached grade level again. If the line is going straight across or the line is going down, the intervention is not working, and you should move on to Tier Two.

Step 5: *Small-Group Intervention (Tier Two)*

Tier Two Interventions are small-group interventions, so they are not delivered to the full class; they're delivered to a small group of students (only students who are unsuccessful in Tier One full-class interventions).

The reason it's called Response to Intervention is because we don't give a test to determine whether a student needs a Tier Two intervention. Instead, we watch how they respond to the Tier One intervention.

Some people call RTI "Response to Instruction" because the first thing you do is watch how a student responds to instruction. You don't give them a static test; you watch them respond to instruction, and if they don't respond to instruction (like other students do), then they need more intensive interventions. That brings us to a Tier Two small-group intervention.

Small-group interventions are done with a small group of students who share a common problem. In a particular class, you might have a group of four students who are having trouble with the beginning sounds of words, or you might have a group of three students who are struggling with their subtraction facts. You might have students who are struggling with reading in a particular area, and these students will get a small-group intervention.

This is delivered perhaps in-class or perhaps out-of-class, perhaps by the classroom teacher or by another qualified adult, perhaps in addition to instruction, and perhaps instead of the core instruction.

The small-group intervention is a research-proven intervention. This means that there is an independent study showing that this intervention has been shown to improve the specific problem that we're trying to address. It is very important that you match the Tier Two small-group intervention with the deficiency that the student has, specifically what they're struggling with, and that the intervention has been shown to solve that problem.

Step 6: *Small-Group Intervention Fidelity Check*

During the Tier Two small-group intervention, you want to do a Fidelity Check—that means to have another adult come into the room and watch to make sure that the intervention is being delivered correctly.

That adult should check for two things: they should check for the process (how it is being delivered—is it being taught correctly?) and dosage. Dosage means is it being given in the correct quantity?

Even the best intervention doesn't work if it's only delivered five minutes a week. Each intervention has been research-proven to work at a specific dosage. For some interventions, 20 minutes a day, 3 days a week is enough. For other interventions, 30 minutes a day, 4 days a week is enough. Some interventions need 45 minutes a day, 5 days a week.

So you want to check these two things. First, is the intervention being delivered correctly? Is it being taught correctly, the way that it was research-proven to work? And second, is it being delivered at the correct dosage?

You want to make sure that you document this Fidelity Check. What we are doing is creating a set of paperwork that is moving along with the student as they move through the RTI process.

What's the first piece of paperwork? The first piece of paperwork was the Universal Screening results.

What's the second piece of paperwork? That's the full-class intervention – what curriculum was being taught.

What's the third piece of paperwork? It's the Fidelity Check—the written documentation of the full-class intervention observation.

The fourth piece of paperwork is the graph from the progress monitoring during Tier One.

And the fifth piece of paperwork is the small-group intervention and the Fidelity Check of that small-group intervention.

People often ask, "How do you not get overwhelmed with the paperwork that comes with RTI?"

Well, you prevent overwhelm by creating a simple system of managing paperwork. In my model of RTI, I am able to take a student from non-identified through ready for identification for special education in less than nine pieces of paper. You don't get overwhelmed with paperwork because you have a limited number of students that you're doing this with, and it's just a few pieces of paper for each student.

Now, I know many of you are struggling with Response to Intervention right now because you're in systems that require piles and piles of paper. Those systems are designed for failure.

Until you are serious about simplifying the RTI process, it is not going to be implemented fully at your school, because teachers simply will not fully embrace a system that creates so much paperwork that it is unmanageable.

Step 7: Small-Group Intervention Progress Monitoring

The next step of Response to Intervention is the progress monitoring during Tier Two.

The progress monitoring during Tier Two is done with every student who is in the Tier Two small-group intervention.

It is usually conducted at the same time, in the same place, and by the same person who is delivering the intervention. Again, you can do your progress monitoring 2 to 3 times per week.

Record the results and graph them, and when you have 10 to 12 results over a period of 4 to 6 weeks, you are ready to make a decision.

At decision-making time, you connect your 12 dots and you look at the line. If the line's going up, the intervention is working, and you should keep doing the intervention until the student is at the level that you are satisfied with, usually back at grade level. If the intervention isn't working, if the line's going straight across or down, then you are ready to move up to the next level.

Step 8: *Tier Three*

The next level is Tier Three, and in some states using a three-tier model and some districts using a three-tier model, Tier Three is when we are ready to look at Special Education Services or eligibility for Special Education Services.

In other states using a four-tier or five-tier model, Tier Three is similar to Tier Two—it's a small group or one-on-one intervention—it's just more intensive (a smaller number of students per teacher and more frequent intervention). Instead of three days a week, it's five days a week. Instead of 30 minutes a day, it's 50 minutes a day.

If you are in a three-tier model, you're at the point where you're ready to determine eligibility for Special

Education. If you are not—if you're in a four-tier model or a give-tier model—you're going to repeat the small-group intervention process again until you get to the eligibility for Special Education decision. Tier Three in a three-tier model is Special Education Services.

Schools use Response to Intervention for two reasons. Some schools use Response to Intervention simply to help students who need help. RTI is *good teaching*. It helps deliver needed services to students who need extra help.

Other schools use RTI as part of the Special Education eligibility process, and I highly recommend that you do this at your school and in your district. It is one of the best uses of Response to Intervention, and it is originally why it was written into No Child Left Behind.

Conclusion

This is a simple explanation of Response to Intervention. You'll notice I didn't show you any pictures of triangles or pyramids, because, in my estimation, they do not help teachers understand Response to Intervention.

What helps teachers understand Response to Intervention is when you tell them they are already doing the Universal Screening, they are already doing full-class intervention/instruction, and they are already being observed during this full-class instruction.

All we want you to add is monitoring the progress of a few students during that instruction to see if it's working, and if it's not, we'll try some small-group interventions and monitor their progress during them, which will lead you to a decision on eligibility for Special Education Services.

Explained this way, teachers go from resisting Response to Intervention to embracing Response to Intervention.

Explained in a simple way, RTI doesn't seem overwhelming; it seems doable. In addition to this, when you simplify the paperwork, it goes from a massive amount of extra paperwork that overwhelms teachers to a simple set of forms that are filled out very naturally during the process. At the end of the process, we have less than nine pieces of paper that we can use to help determine eligibility for Special Education Services, or what the next correct step is for each student.

That's a simple explanation for Response to Intervention.

Is it as complicated as others? No.

Is it as comprehensive as others? No.

Why do we use this simple explanation? Because if you don't, RTI won't be implemented fully at your schools.

Teachers will drag their feet, teachers will put it off, teachers will say they're doing it when they're not, because they are scared, overwhelmed, and buried in paperwork.

Remember this: Simpler is better when explaining Response to Intervention to your teachers.

Appendix C

ADDITIONAL READING
AND RESOURCES

Adams, C. M., & Pierce, R. L. (2010). *Differentiation that really works, grades 3-5: Strategies from real teachers for real classrooms.* Waco, TX: Prufrock.

Allen, L., & Evans, J. (1994). *First Steps: oral language developmental continuum.* Portsmouth, NH: Heinemann.

Angell, C. A., & Hartwig, E. P. (2006). *Evidence-based education: examining today's research for tomorrow's decisions.* Horsham, PA: LRP Publications.

Bender, W. N. (2008). *Differentiating instruction for students with learning disabilities* (2nd ed.). Thousand Oaks, CA: Corwin.

Boyles, N. N. (2011). *Rethinking small-group instruction.* Gainesville, FL: Maupin House Publishing.

Brown-Chidsey, R., & Steege, M. W. (2005). *Response to intervention: principles and strategies for effective practice.* New York: The Guilford Press.

DeBaryshe, B. D., Gorecki, D. M., & Mishima-Young, L. N. (2009). *Differentiated instruction to support high-risk preschool learners. NHSA Dialog: A Research-to-Practice Journal for the Early Intervention Field,* 12(3), 227–244.

Fattig, M. L., & Taylor, M. T. (2008). *Co-teaching in the differentiated classroom: Successful collaboration, lesson design, and classroom management: Grades 5–12.* San Francisco: Jossey-Bass.

Gent, P. J. (2009). *Great ideas: Using service-learning and differentiated instruction to help your students succeed.* Baltimore, MD: Paul H. Brookes.

Gore, M. C. (Ed.). (2010). *Inclusion strategies for secondary classrooms: Keys for struggling learners* (2nd ed.). Thousand Oaks, CA: Corwin.

Gregory, G. H., & Kuzmich, L. (2010). *Student teams that get results: Teaching tools for the differentiated classroom.* Thousand Oaks, CA: Corwin.

Gregory, G. H., & Kuzmich, L. (2005). *Differentiated learning strategies for student growth and achievement in grades 7-12.* Thousand Oaks, CA: Corwin Press.

Haager, D., Klingner, J., & Vaughn, S. (2007). *Evidence-based reading practices for response to intervention.* Baltimore: Paul H. Brookes Publishing Co.

Hamm, M., & Adams, D. (2008). *Differentiated instruction for K-8 math and science: Activities and lesson plans.* Larchmont, NY: Eye On Education.

Hardcastle, B., & Justice, K. (2006). *RtI and the classroom teacher: a guide for fostering teacher buy-in and supporting the intervention process.* West Palm Beach, FL: LRP Publications.

Harp, B. (2005). *The informed teacher: research-based practice.* Upper Saddle River, NJ: Prentice Hall.

King-Sears, M. E. (2008). *Facts and fallacies: Differentiation and the general education curriculum for students with special educational needs. Support for Learning,* 23(2), 55–62.

Lane, K. L., & Beebe-Frankenberger, M. (2004). *School-based interventions: the tools you need to succeed.* Boston: Pearson Education, Inc.

Lalley, J. P., & Gentile, R. (2009). *Adapting instruction to individuals: based on the evidence, What should it mean? International Journal of Teaching and Learning in Higher Education,* 20(3), 462-475.

Larner, M. (1995). *Linking family and early childhood programs: issues, experiences, opportunities.* Chicago: Family resource coalition.

Lenz, B. K. (2004). *Teaching content to all: evidence-based inclusion practices in middle and secondary schools.* Boston: Allyn and Bacon.

Manning, S., Stanford, B., & Reeves, S. (2010). *Valuing the advanced learner: Differentiating up. Clearing House: A Journal of Educational Strategies, Issues and Ideas,* 83(4), 145–149.

Marzano, R. J. (2010). *High expectations for all.* Educational Leadership, 68(1), 82–84.

Middendorf, C. (2008). *Differentiating instruction in kindergarten.* New York: Scholastic.

Narvaez, L., & Brimijoin, K. (2010). *Differentiation at work, K-5: Principles, lessons, and strategies.* Thousand Oaks, CA: Corwin.

Quinn, Patrick. (2009). *Ultimate RTI: What Every Teacher Needs to Know to Implement Response to Intervention.* Slinger, WI: Ideas Unlimited Seminars, Inc.

Roberts, J. L., & Inman, T. F. (2007). *Strategies for differentiating instruction: Best practices for the classroom.* Waco, TX: Prufrock.

Shapiro, E. S. (2004). *Academic skills problems: direct assessment and intervention.* New York: The Guilford Press.

Shute, V. J., & Becker, B. J. (Eds.). (2010). *Innovative assessment for the 21st century: Supporting educational needs.* New York: Springer.

Slobof, J. (1999). *Providing cross-cultural support services to individuals with disabilities and their families.* Minneapolis: Institute on Community Integration.

Sondergeld, T. A., & Schultz, A. (2008). *Science, standards, and differentiation: It really can be fun!* Gifted Child Today, 31(1), 34–40.

Sprague, J. R. (2005). *Safe and healthy schools: practical prevention strategies.* New York: The Guilford Press.

Thousand, J. S., Villa, R. A., & Nevin, A. I. (2007). *Differentiating instruction: Collaborative planning and teaching for universally designed learning.* Thousand Oaks, CA: Corwin.

Tomlinson, C. A., & McTighe, J. (2006). *Integrating differentiated instruction & understanding by design.* Alexandria, VA: Association for Supervision and Curriculum Development.

Walpole, S., & McKenna, M. C. (2007). *Differentiated reading instruction: Strategies for the primary grades.* New York: Guilford.

Wheeler, J. J. (2005). *Behavior management: principles and practices of positive behavior supports.* Upper Saddle River, NJ: Prentice Hall.

Williams, L. (2008). *Tiering and scaffolding: Two strategies for providing access to important mathematics.* Teaching Children Mathematics, 14(6), 324–330.

Wolfgang, C. H., Bennett, B., & Irvin, J. L. (1999). *Strategies for teaching self-discipline in the middle grades.* Needham Heights, MA: Allyn and Bacon.

Zirkel, P. A. (2006). *The legal meaning of specific learning disability for special education eligibility.* Arlington, VA: Council for Exceptional Children.

ABOUT PAT QUINN
"THE RTI GUY!"

Pat Quinn has spent his entire career helping struggling students become successful in school. As a teacher, author, and nationally recognized keynote speaker, he has changed thousands of lives through his insightful message. Pat Quinn helps educators around the country improve their teaching, renew their passion, and lengthen their careers as he speaks about closing the achievement gap and meeting the needs of all students.

Mr. Quinn is the author of twelve books on meeting the individual needs of students, including *Ultimate RTI*, *Designing an Alternative Curriculum*, *Helping Hispanic Students Succeed* and the bestselling *Changing Lives*. He has taught undergraduate courses for Lakeland College and graduate courses at Alverno College. He is the former editor of the educational newsletter *The Unconventional Teacher*.

To subscribe to Pat Quinn's RTI newsletter, visit:

www.response-to-intervention.com

Email Pat Quinn at: pat@betterteachingonline.com

Made in the USA
Lexington, KY
28 July 2015